BOB GO

EVERYBODY ALWAYS

BECOMING LOVE in a
WORLD FULL *of* SETBACKS
and DIFFICULT PEOPLE

NELSON
BOOKS

An Imprint of Thomas Nelson

Published in Nashville, Tennessee, by Nelson Books, an imprint of Thomas Nelson. Nelson Books and Thomas Nelson are registered trademarks of HarperCollins Christian Publishing, Inc.

The author is represented by Alive Literary Agency, 7680 Goddard Street, Suite 200, Colorado Springs, CO 80920, www.aliveliterary.com.

Thomas Nelson titles may be purchased in bulk for educational, business, fund-raising, or sales promotional use. For information, please email SpecialMarkets@ThomasNelson.com.

The quotation in "My Bucket" is taken from *How Full Is Your Bucket? For Kids* by Tom Rath.

Unless otherwise noted, Scripture quotations are taken from THE HOLY BIBLE, NEW INTERNATIONAL VERSION®, NIV® Copyright © 1973, 1978, 1984, 2011 by Biblica, Inc.® Used by permission. All rights reserved worldwide.

Scripture quotation in chapter 15 is taken from the *Holy Bible*, New Living Translation, copyright © 1996, 2004, 2015 by Tyndale House Foundation. Used by permission of Tyndale House Publishers Inc., Carol Stream, Illinois 60188. All rights reserved.

Any Internet addresses, phone numbers, or company or product information printed in this book are offered as a resource and are not intended in any way to be or to imply an endorsement by Thomas Nelson, nor does Thomas Nelson vouch for the existence, content, or services of these sites, phone numbers, companies, or products beyond the life of this book.

ISBN 978-0-7180-7813-3 (TP)
ISBN 978-1-4002-1056-5 (signed edition)
ISBN 978-0-7180-7817-1 (eBook)

Library of Congress Control Number: 2017956051

Printed in the United States of America
18 19 20 21 22 LSC 13

I've spent my whole life trying to make my faith easy. The truth is, it's not. From what I've been reading, if we do it right, it will actually kill all the earlier versions of us. What I'm trying to do now is make my faith simple.

This book is dedicated to everyone who has helped my friends and me make faith increasingly simple. These people haven't tried to save up love like they're going to need it later; they know we're rivers, not reservoirs. It's also a really long thank-you note to everyone who has ever done something nice for Sweet Maria, for one of my kids, or for someone they love. When you've done it for them, you've done it for me. I know God feels the same way.

CONTENTS

CONTENTS

PROLOGUE

I wrote a book called *Love Does* a few years ago. We took all the money from the book and opened schools and safe houses, homes for abandoned infants, and orphanages in Somalia, Uganda, Iraq, Nepal, and other countries where regional conflicts have endangered the children living there. It was my first shot at writing a book, and I tried to tell stories of some things I've learned about the immense power love has in the world. There was supposed to be a second book, but it was never published. This is my third book. Let me tell you why.

A number of years ago, a friend of mine quit the megachurch he pastored in Southern California and moved to the inner city of San Francisco. He wanted to build a community among people who had experienced tremendous failures and setbacks. He's a humble guy, is generous with his time, loves his family, and really loves God. Rather than spend only a few minutes each week with the thousands of people at the big church he pastored for years, he decided to go deep with a small number of people who had faced some tough breaks. He and a few friends started a restaurant staffed by guys who needed a fresh start and also a home for women who have confronted some of life's biggest challenges with courage and hope.

These amazing people spend their free time loving people in the housing projects near the restaurant. They give away love like they're made of it. Like my friend, they do this because they have developed completely unrealistic ideas about what their faith can do in the world when it's expressed in love. They decided to spend more time loving people than trying to game the system by just agreeing with Jesus. You see, they wanted to follow Jesus' example; instead of telling people what Jesus meant, they just loved people the way He did.

The housing projects are difficult places. They're dark and scary and filled with beautiful, scary people. They are full of guns and violence and fights and theft. They are also full of love and compassion and generosity and hope.

These brave men and women from the restaurant seek out people who have felt forgotten and overlooked. They pursue the wrongdoers and disadvantaged and discouraged, and they love them Jesus-style—with extravagant grace.

On one of the trips to see my friend in San Francisco, I brought a couple of people who work with me. We flew in, rented a van, and headed over to the restaurant to see how we could help. We had been inside washing dishes for about thirty minutes when I went outside to get something out of the van. I was drop-jawed at what I found. All the windows were shattered, pieces of glass scattered on the seats and floorboards. Thieves in the neighborhood had broken in. All our luggage was gone. Oh, and our wallets, cell phones, and laptop computers too.

I had just finished writing the first draft of this book, and it was on my stolen computer. Get this: the manuscript wasn't backed up. (Who needs iCloud? It costs ninety-nine cents a month.) Minor oversight on my part. I had to write the book all over again.

The good news was that I had been thinking about this book's idea for a while. A few years earlier, I had been with some dear friends at a large church in Chicago and gave a sermon where I said we need to love everybody, always. It made sense to me, so I decided to write a book about it.

It's hard to believe Jesus loves the van thieves and all the difficult people we've met just the same as you and me. Yet, the incredible message Love came to earth to give was that we're all tied for first in God's mind. While we're still trying to get our arms around this idea, God doesn't want us to just study Him like He's an academic project. He wants us to become love.

I've heard it's hard to write a good second book and that they usually stink. The thieves probably did us all a favor, so let's just call this my third book. It's given me a lot of comfort knowing we're all rough drafts of the people we're still becoming. I hope this second version of the book moves the needle in a way that reaffirms the power of extravagant love and excessive grace in your life and in the world.

CHAPTER 1

Creepy People

*We don't need to be who we used to
be; God sees who we're becoming—
and we're becoming love.*

My friends and I finished what we were doing at the restaurant and took the windowless van back to the airport. We pulled into the rental lot looking a little windblown, and the attendant stared at us with a puzzled expression. "It looked like this when we got it," I told him nonchalantly. Walking away, I tossed the keys to him. I felt like the guy in the movies when he throws a match over his shoulder and the car explodes behind him. Pro tip: If you do throw the match, make sure you don't turn around and look when it blows up. It wrecks the vibe.

I was disappointed everything was stolen, but I figured it would all work out. What I didn't realize was how hard it would be to get back on an airplane to fly home with no identification. I got to the front of the security line, and the guy with a badge asked for my ticket and ID. I reached in my pockets and turned them inside out. I had nothing. I shrugged my shoulders pathetically and said, "Man, it all got stolen. My luggage, my wallet, everything." I felt like Jason Bourne.

The TSA guy wasn't very sympathetic. I could understand. He was just doing his job. He asked if there was any way I could prove who I was. I shook my head, then suddenly remembered—I had written a book a while ago. We Googled it, but I forgot the cover only had balloons on it. (I made a mental note to put a huge photo of myself on the cover of this book just in case it happens again, but I bailed on the idea when I saw what my face looked like on a book cover.)

All of this raised a question I've been thinking about a lot lately. *How do we prove who we are?* I don't mean who our driver's licenses say we are or what our careers suggest about who we are or who we tell other people we are or who they tell us we are. Jesus talked to His friends a lot about how we should identify ourselves. He said it wouldn't be what we said we believed or all the good we hoped to do someday. Nope, He said we would identify ourselves simply by how we loved people. It's tempting to think there is more to it, but there's not. Love isn't something we fall into; love is someone we become.

It's easy to love kind, lovely, humble people. I mean, who wouldn't? These are the ones I've spent much of my life loving. Loving the people who are easy to love made me feel like I was really good at it. Because the people I loved were kind and wonderful, they made sure they told me what a great job I was doing loving them. What I've come to realize, though, is that I was avoiding the people I didn't understand and the ones who lived differently than me. Here's why: some of them creeped me out. Sure, I was polite to them, but sadly, I've spent my whole life avoiding the people Jesus spent His whole life engaging. God's idea isn't that we would just give and receive love but that we could actually *become love*. People who are becoming love see the beauty in others even when their off-putting behavior makes for a pretty weird mask. What Jesus told His friends can be summed up in this way: He wants us to love everybody, always—and start with the people who creep us out. The truth is, we probably creep them out as much as they do us.

Are there people you should give a wide berth to? You bet. There are people in my life and yours who are unsafe, toxic, and delight in sowing discord wherever they go. God gave us discernment, and we should use it as we live our lives. He's also given us love and understanding and kindness and the ability to forgive, which have power we often leave untapped. There's a difference between good judgment and living in judgment. The trick is to use lots of the first and to go a little lighter on the second.

What I'm learning about love is that we have to tackle a good amount of fear to love people who are difficult. Oftentimes, when I encounter someone who makes me feel afraid, I instantly put up barriers. I put them up with my big words and opinions. I construct them to protect myself. Barriers make me feel right, and that makes me feel safe. I think this is something we all do to some degree, and there's no shame in that. Except it's not what Jesus did.

He showed us what it means to become love when He spent His last meal with a man who He knew would betray Him and then willingly died a criminal's death.

We make loving people a lot more complicated than Jesus did. Every time I try to protect myself by telling somebody about one of my opinions, God whispers to me and asks about my heart. *Why are you so afraid? Who are you trying to impress?* Am I really so insecure that I surround myself only with people who agree with me? When people are flat wrong, why do I appoint myself the sheriff to straighten them out? Burning down others' opinions doesn't make us right. It makes us arsonists.

God's endgame has always been the same. He wants our hearts to be His. He wants us to love the people near us and love the people we've kept far away. To do this, He wants us to live without fear. We don't need to use our opinions to mask our insecurities anymore. Instead, God wants us to grow love in our hearts and then cultivate it by the acre in the world. We'll become in our lives what we do with our love. Those who are becoming love don't throw people off roofs; they lower people through them instead.

In high school, someone asked me if I had "met Jesus." I thought he was kidding. "Of course not," I answered literally. I still haven't. I don't have any friends who have either. From what I've read, very few people on this side of heaven have actually ever met God. Adam and Eve did. Joseph and Mary did too. Moses did on the top of a mountain. Some shepherds and a few wise men make the list. A boatful of fishermen, a couple of thieves on a hill. There were plenty of others, but not as many as you might think.

By contrast, there were a lot of people who watched Jesus from a distance. He walked their streets and went to their parties. He stood before leaders, and a few even saw Him raised up on a cross. I suppose they could say they met Him, but at best, they probably just got a glimpse of Him. For a long time, I saw Jesus from a distance and thought we'd met. It still happens to me every time I avoid people God made in His own image just because I don't understand them. My fear of them leaves me only with glimpses of Jesus. What I've come to realize is if I really want to "meet Jesus," then I have to get a lot closer to the people He created. All of them, not just some of them.

God could have made it otherwise, of course, and everyone could have actually met Jesus. He could have appeared in person throughout history in all maternity wards and huts and fields where children are born. He could have shown up at Super Bowl games and Taylor Swift concerts and at elementary school plays and the Rose Parade. By not doing this, I don't think He's avoiding us. I think His plan all along has been for us to meet the people He made and feel like we just met Him.

In this sense, I've met God almost every day. Certainly, God wants us to learn about Him by reading the letters and stories collected in the Bible, but He also wants us to meet Him by loving the people who are difficult to get along with. If I'm only willing to love the people who are nice to me, the ones who see things the way I do, and avoid all the rest, it's like reading every other page of the Bible and thinking I know what it says.

Jesus told His friends if they wanted to be like Him, they needed to love their neighbors and they needed to love difficult people. This sounds so familiar that I'm tempted to just agree with Jesus and move on, but Jesus doesn't want us merely to agree with Him. In fact, I can't think of a single time He gathered His friends around Him and said, "Guys, I just want you to agree with Me." He wants us to do what He said, and He said He wants us to love everybody, always.

Jesus said to love our enemies. I thought I'd get off easy because I don't have any real "enemies." I mean, I'm not mad at North Korea or Russia or China. And I don't think they're mad at me. After all, I wrote a book and put balloons on the cover. Who could be mad at that guy? I think Jesus meant something different when He said "enemies." He meant we should love the people we don't understand. The ones we disagree with. The ones who are flat wrong about more than a couple of things. I have plenty of those people in my life, and my bet is you do too. In fact, I might be one of those people sometimes.

I think God allows all of us to go missing a time or two. He doesn't lose us like I did my computer when my van was broken into, but He lets us get lost for a while if it's what we really want. When we do, He doesn't pout or withhold His love the way I probably would if someone completely ignored me or walked away from me. Instead, He pursues us in love. He's not trying to find us; He always knows where we are. Rather, He goes *with* us as we find ourselves again. In this way, we have both a little sheep and some shepherd in us too. God isn't constantly telling us what to do as we search for ourselves either. He gently reminds us who we are. He continues to rewrite our lives the way I rewrote my book—in beautiful and unexpected ways, knowing the next version of us will usually be better than the previous one.

As a lawyer, I win arguments for a living, but something has changed within me. I want to be Jesus. I've concluded we can be correct and not right. Know what I mean? I do this most often when I have the right words and the wrong heart. Sadly, whenever I make my opinions more important than the difficult people God made, I turn the wine back into water. I'm trying to resist the bait that darkness offers me every day to trade kindness for rightness. These are not mutually exclusive ideas, of course, but there's a big difference between being kind and being right. Pick the most controversial social issue of the day, and you'll find passionate voices on all sides. The sad fact is, many of us have lost our way trying to help people find theirs. Arguments won't change people. Simply giving away kindness won't either. Only Jesus has the power to change people, and it will be harder for them to see Jesus if their view of Him is blocked by our big opinions.

I used to think we'd be known for whom we hung around, the groups or social issues we identified with, or the faith tradition we were familiar with. Now I think while we might be known for our opinions, we'll be remembered for our love. What I've learned following Jesus is we only really find our identities by engaging the people we've been avoiding. Jesus wrapped up this concept in three simple and seemingly impossible ideas for us to follow: love Him, love your neighbor, and love your enemies.

I want to love God more fully. I really do. Who wouldn't? I want to love my neighbors too. Why not? I live next door to some of them. Overall, they are kind of like me. But love my enemies? Sure, I'll tolerate them for a while. I might even be nice to them for a couple of minutes. But *love* them? Yikes.

In the simplest terms, Jesus came to earth and declared He would turn God's enemies into His friends. He didn't do it with twenty-dollar words or lectures or by waving a bony finger at people who had made mistakes. He convinces us with love, and He does it without fear or shame. He doesn't raise His voice and shout over the noise in our lives. He lets the power of love do all the talking for Him. We have the same shot in other people's lives every day.

Loving each other is what we were meant to do and how we were made to roll. It's not where we start when we begin following Jesus; it's the beautiful path we travel the rest of our lives. Will it be messy and ambiguous and uncomfortable when we love people the way Jesus said to love them? You bet it will. Will we be misunderstood? Constantly. But extravagant love often means coloring outside the lines and going beyond the norms. Loving the neighbors we don't understand takes work and humility and patience and guts. It means leaving the security of our easy relationships to engage in some tremendously awkward ones.

Find a way to love difficult people more, and you'll be living the life Jesus talked about. Go find someone you've been avoiding and give away extravagant love to them. You'll learn more about God, your neighbor, your enemies, and your faith. Find someone you think is wrong, someone you disagree with, someone who isn't like you at all, and decide to love that person the way you want Jesus to love you.

We need to love everybody, always.

Jesus never said doing these things would be easy. He just said it would work.

CHAPTER 2

Meeting Carol

God doesn't just give us promises;
He gives us each other.

Shortly after Sweet Maria and I got married, we bought our first home. We got it at a foreclosure sale. It was more my idea than hers. Walking through the house after we bought it was the closest thing I've had to a near-death experience. Sweet Maria looked at me with her hands in her pockets and nodded in disbelief as we walked from room to room. Unconvincingly and with a hint of uncharacteristic sarcasm, she looked inside each of the ramshackle rooms and said, "Nice" from time to time as she shook her head in absolute denial. Translated, that meant, "We're still married, but just barely."

The house was in terrible shape. It was so nasty, the mice reported us. Rather than move in, we lived in a motor home in the driveway while we made it habitable. After waking up with a steering wheel and a parking brake in our bedroom for a year, we decided we'd take a step down in our lifestyle and move from the car to the house. There was a heater, but it didn't work. There was a bathroom, but it didn't work either. The house came with twenty feral cats that were apparently afraid of rodents but not afraid to shed. With a spinning wheel and enough allergy medicine, I could have made a hundred really gross sweaters with all the cat hair we collected.

On the day of the move, I picked up Sweet Maria and carried her across the threshold. As I did, we both saw something move in the corner of the living room but pretended we didn't. This house wasn't much, but it was ours.

We fixed up the house and swapped it for another house and then another and then another. During the first ten years we were married, we moved six times. It was like being in the witness protection program, but we hadn't done anything wrong. After many moves and remodels, we were exhausted. One day after work, I drove home to the wrong house and walked in the front door. It was more than a little weird for a couple of minutes.

A short time later, I was at breakfast with a friend and overheard a guy in the next booth say he was planning on selling his house. I eavesdropped a little more on their conversation and learned his house was at the top of a cliff, right above my favorite surfing spot in Point Loma called Garbage Beach. Who wouldn't want a house there, right?

I slid into the booth next to the guy and told him I wanted his house. We worked out all the details over waffles. I made a really lame move and threw in our china to seal the deal. *Sweet Maria's going to love it*, I thought as I drove home from the restaurant, having just traded the house she had poured her heart into for years for a house at a place called Garbage. I blindfolded Sweet Maria and drove her to our new home. I did the big reveal when we got there. I pointed to my surf spot and then back toward the house a couple of times. I asked if she could believe what a smart guy I was.

She started quietly crying and told me in a very kind but direct voice that every marriage gets one of these kinds of mistakes. I had just used mine up. We moved in, and she did the same thing she does in the lives of people around her. She took the garbage I brought and transformed it into a life and a home for our young family. Our children had arrived two years apart up until that point. There was a much larger gap before our last child arrived.

Unfortunately, it wouldn't be my last mistake. A short time later, we bought another house, this time at a probate court auction. The auction was held at the courthouse, and quite a few people came to bid on the house. I've always had trouble sitting still, and while I was at the auction I pulled on my ear, scratched my chin, and wrinkled my nose. When I was done fidgeting, I guess we'd outbid everyone, so we ended up with the house.

A few years later, Sweet Maria told me she wanted to move from the house we were living in. There was a long, awkward pause while I mustered up the courage to sheepishly ask, "Can I come?" It's one of the few rules in our marriage—we agreed if Sweet Maria ever decides to leave me, she has to take me with her.

I started getting caught up in Sweet Maria's excitement about moving again and pointed at the house across the street. "That one's for sale. What if we move there?" Maria thought I was just too cheap to get a moving van, but the truth was—I was just too cheap to get a moving van. We bought it and put a For Sale sign in the front yard of our previous home to see what would happen. Within a day or two, five people wanted to buy our house. Because we were moving across the street, we weren't just looking for a buyer; we were looking for a neighbor. There's a big difference. You do business with buyers; you do life with neighbors.

We started boxing up our things. We put the small items in red wagons and wheelbarrows and put roller skates and skateboards under the bigger things like refrigerators and washing machines and me. All the while, we continued to interview people for the job of being our new neighbor.

Because I'm a diplomat for the Republic of Uganda, the last thing we did when we moved in across the street was to raise the Ugandan flag over our new home. Not many people know this, but where the consul lives and the flag of Uganda flies, it's actually Ugandan soil. It's hard to believe, but our house is the diplomatic mission of a foreign country to the United States. I suppose if you mess up big enough in your life, you could come over and seek asylum at my house. When things happen at our home now, we don't call the police. We call the Feds, and agents come within minutes. I've only called once, but it's pretty cool.

After meeting all the people who wanted to buy our home, our family unanimously picked Carol to be our neighbor. She was a standout. Carol was a widow in her early fifties. She was moving to San Diego to be closer to her family and was hoping to live near the Bay. The Bible talks a lot about how we should care for widows. I don't think God did this just to be nice to them. I bet He knew we'd find out a great deal about ourselves if we did. We gave Carol a group hug as we all said, "Carol, welcome to the neighborhood." A few weeks later, we found ourselves in the blast radius of her stunning love and kindness.

As they grew up, our kids would run across the street to Carol's house to show her their art projects or tell her stories about how we used to let them play dodgeball in the hallway, having coined the game "hall-ball." They told her how our son Richard lost a frog in the living room and how our daughter, Lindsey, once officiated her brother Adam's marriage to a life-size Barbie at the house when he was four. With each story, Carol would put her hand to her mouth to half-cover genuine expressions of wonder and amazement while giggling like a schoolgirl. Never satisfied with the kids' first attempt at their stories, she would beg them to tell her more—usually about the frog that got away. All the while, she would feed them mountains of cookies. Years later, when Richard married Ashley in our backyard, Carol sat next to us in the front row. She wasn't just a neighbor; she had become part of our family.

In the decades that passed after we gave Carol the house keys, I would call her a couple of times a week to see how she was doing. My phone calls to check on Carol were never long, but they were always meaningful. One day, I called Carol to see how she was doing, and she struck an uncharacteristically serious tone. Her voice broke a little as she said, "Bob, I just got back from the doctor, and she gave me some bad news. I have cancer." Her words hung over the phone like they were stuck in the wires. I was sad for Carol and could tell she was terrified. I thought for a second, then said, "Carol, I'm coming over with something." No doubt, she was a little puzzled.

I rushed to RadioShack and got us two walkie-talkies. I set up one next to Carol's bed, and I set up the other one next to ours. Carol and I started talking exclusively on walkie-talkies. The first time I called her over the radio waves, I said, "Hello, Carol?" The walkie-talkie made that static sound they make in the movies. A few long seconds later, Carol's voice came crackling over the radio. "Bob, is that you?" I laughed as I thought, *Who else would it be?*

Something happens when you're talking on walkie-talkies. You get the same feeling when you connect two peach cans together with a string—you're both instantly transformed into nine-year-olds. No one has cancer, nobody is alone, and no one is terrified anymore. Our houses became the tree forts; walkie-talkies were the cans. Carol and I talked for the next couple of years on the walkie-talkies. These walkie-talkies didn't fix her cancer. Something much bigger happened—she wasn't afraid anymore.

When some of Jesus' friends were arguing about who would get to sit closer to Him when they got to heaven, Jesus told them unless they changed and became like children, they'd never enter the kingdom of God. I think what He was saying is we need a childlike faith to understand Him. That makes a lot of sense to me. It's not acting childish that will get us to heaven. Plenty of people do that. It won't be our big prayers and fancy language that will help us get there either. Big faith doesn't need big words. We also don't need to make faith easier, because it's not; we need to make it simpler, because it is. Children have mastered what most of us are just beginners at. One of the things about kids, in addition to their simple faith, is they aren't afraid of the things many of us are afraid of. Their curiosity about what they don't know outdistances their fears about what they do know by a mile.

Three words stand out to me in the Bible. They aren't big and deep and theological words, yet that's probably what makes them big and deep and theological in nature. Here they are: *Be. Not. Afraid.* God whispered, *Be not afraid* to Joshua when he didn't think he was the right guy to take over for Moses; He shouted those same words to Abram before a big battle when He said He'd be his shield and great reward; and Jesus said these words confidently to a boatful of scared fishermen when He walked out to them on the water. *Be. Not. Afraid.* These words have exactly as much power as we give them in our lives. People who are becoming love experience the same uncertainties we all do. They just stop letting fear call the shots.

If we take to heart Jesus' words about having a childlike faith and not being afraid, they can move us from merely wishing things would get better for us to bearing up under the circumstances God actually gives us. They let us move from running away and hiding from our problems to engaging and embracing them. These words can fill us with quiet confidence and contagious hope. What's crazy is when we're not afraid and engage the world with a child-like faith, the people around us won't be afraid either. Hope and courage do the same things. When we let them, they'll spread like a cold. A really good kind of cold.

Carol began a long and ferocious fight with cancer, which had laid claim to many parts of her body. But cancer could never touch her spirit for one simple reason: she wasn't afraid anymore. She was playing offense, not defense.

I gave Carol a ride to one of her chemotherapy treatments. We sat in heated chairs next to each other and laughed a lot. I brought little colored umbrellas to put in the chemo bags and asked the nurse to hook me up with a bag of my own. Carol and I pretended we were in Hawaii, sitting by a pool. When you're together with someone you love, you get to decide where you are, even if it's different from where you actually are.

Carol made huge progress in the fight of her life, and she had more than a few setbacks too. During one of the turns she took early on, she ended up in the hospital for an emergency operation. After her surgery, I went to the recovery room. A snarl of tubes disappeared under the curtain surrounding Carol's bed. I found the nurse who was looking after Carol, turned on a walkie-talkie, and gave it to her to take to Carol. I snuck in and lay down on the other bed in her room behind my own curtain.

I sat quietly for several minutes and asked God again if He'd heal my friend and let her live. Then I turned on my walkie-talkie and whispered into it, "Hello, Carol?" It made the crackling static sound again. There was a long silence, and I could hear some fumbling around on Carol's side of the curtain. Then a weak voice said, "Hello, Bob? Is that you?" We both laid our heads back on our pillows and laughed through the tears.

CHAPTER 3

Love Everybody, Always

*"Love one another." What is simple often
isn't easy; what is easy often doesn't last.*

It was a lawyer like me who tried to set up Jesus. This law-yer asked Jesus what the greatest commandment was. I think he was looking for a plan, but Jesus told him about his purpose instead. He said it was to love God with all his heart and soul and mind. Then in the next breath, Jesus gave the lawyer some unsolicited but practical advice. Jesus told him he should love his neighbors just like he loved himself. Sometimes we see these as two separate ideas, but Jesus saw loving God and loving our neighbors as one inseparable mandate. They were tied for first in Jesus' mind. I think Jesus said these things because He knew we couldn't love God if we don't love the people He surrounds us with. Simply put, we can stop waiting for a plan and just go love everybody. There's no school to learn how to love your neighbor, just the house next door. No one expects us to love them flawlessly, but we can love them fearlessly, furiously, and unreasonably.

We're not supposed to love only our neighbors, but Jesus thought we should start with them. I bet He knew if our love isn't going to work for the people who live close to us, then it's probably not going to work for the rest of the world. Jesus didn't say who our neighbors are either. Probably so we wouldn't start making lists of those we don't need to love.

Each of us is surrounded every day by our neighbors. They're ahead of us, behind us, on each side of us. They're every place we go. They're sacking groceries and attending city council meetings. They're holding cardboard signs on street corners and raking leaves next door. They play high school football and deliver the mail. They're heroes and hookers and pastors and pilots. They live on the streets and design our bridges. They go to seminaries and live in prisons. They govern us and they bother us. They're everywhere we look. It's one thing we all have in common: we're all somebody's neighbor, and they're ours. This has been God's simple yet brilliant master plan from the beginning. He made a whole world of neighbors. We call it earth, but God just calls it a really big neighborhood.

What often keeps us from loving our neighbors is fear of what will happen if we do. Frankly, what scares me more is thinking about what will happen if we don't. Being fearless isn't something we can decide to be in a moment, but fear can be overcome with time and the right help. We can bring all the game we've got, but only Jesus has the power to call out of us the kind of courage it takes to live the life He talked about.

For the last twenty-two years, we've put on a New Year's Day parade to celebrate our neighbors. Our parade starts at the cul-de-sac at the end of our block and ends at our front yard. Our whole family wakes up early every year, and we blow up over a thousand helium balloons. We're the reason there's a helium shortage. Before we start taking the balloons out of the house, we give thanks for our neighbors and for the privilege of doing life with them.

Our block has only twenty houses if you count both sides, so our parade isn't a long one. Our first year, there were only eight of us standing at the beginning of the parade route. We stood together at the end of the cul-de-sac, trying to look like a parade. Someone said, "Go," and we started walking down the street and waving to the six neighbors who were watching. Now there are probably four or five hundred people who come each year. Kids pull wagons full of stuffed animals and pet goldfish. There are no fancy floats; bicycles with baseball cards in the spokes are the norm. By the time we all line up for the parade these days, we're already at our house and sometimes a little past it before anyone starts moving.

Here's why we do it: we can't love people we don't know. You can't either. Saying we love our neighbors is simple. But guess what? Doing it is too. Just throw them a parade. We don't think Jesus' command to "love your neighbor" is a metaphor for something else. We think it means we're supposed to actually love our neighbors. Engage them. Delight in them. Throw a party for them. When joy is a habit, love is a reflex.

Because we've been putting on the parade for decades, we know all the people who live near us. I don't know if they've learned anything from us, but we've learned a ton about loving each other from them. God didn't give us neighbors to be our projects; He surrounded us with them to be our teachers.

We don't have a plan for the parade. This cuts down on the preparation time. It's just as well. Love doesn't obey all the rules we try to give it anyway. A week before the parade each year, we knock on a few of our neighbors' front doors and pick a grand marshal and a queen from among them. Being picked as the queen is a big deal in our neighborhood. Carol got the nod one year. A decade later, people still bowed to Carol when they saw her at the corner market or the gas station and called her "Your Majesty." It was just beautiful.

One year, because of the battle raging inside Carol, she didn't think she would be able to walk the parade route from the cul-de-sac to our house where the parade ends. I have an old Harley-Davidson motorcycle with a sidecar. That year, I put Carol in the sidecar and gave her a ride. She was the hit of the parade because all the neighbors knew about the cancer she had been staring down. Carol, elegant as always, waved to everyone, and they waved back. Just before we got to the end of the parade route, Carol turned to me and took a deep, thought-filled breath. It was as if she were going through the highlight reel of her life when she said, "You know, Bob, I'm really going to miss this parade." I looked at my neighbor in the sidecar next to me and said, "Me too, Carol. Me too." Even as I did, I asked God if He would let Carol have at least one more parade with us.

Seven months later, our family had just returned from a trip out of the country. I was with my son Richard when we got the news Carol had gone back into the hospital for another operation. We jumped in the car and hurried to be with her. We moved quickly down the hall and turned into Carol's room just as the doctor was leaving. A somber stillness filled the room as we entered. Carol was propped up in her bed by pillows. Her head was leaned back toward the ceiling. Her eyes were closed, and her hands were folded. The doctor had just told Carol she was going to die. We sat on the bed together, had a good cry, and then we talked about balloons and parades and eternity and Jesus.

Carol came home to the house across the street from us to spend her last days among her friends and neighbors. She had no appetite as her body began shutting down. We were constantly trying to coax her into eating something. Every now and then she would get a bizarre craving for a specific type of food. One day she told me she was itching for a particular kind of hot dog. She went into remarkable detail with me about the width and length and the color of them.

This company must only make about four or five hot dogs a year, because I went to a dozen grocery stores and delis looking for Carol's brand of hot dog with no luck. Eventually, I found a small package. I felt like I had found Jimmy Hoffa. "Yes!" I shouted out from aisle three at the grocery store as I grabbed the package and threw my arms up over my head. I almost spiked them like a football in the end zone but caught myself.

I raced back to Carol's house and opened the package of hot dogs with a reverence reserved for the ark of the covenant. I told Carol I'd bagged the exact one she was craving. Carol told me she wanted to see the wrapper. Even in her weakened condition she wanted to make sure we hadn't gone Oscar Mayer on her.

Carol couldn't eat much more than a teaspoonful of food at any time. Sweet Maria mocked up the king of all hot dogs for her to look at and piled it high with the works. It had a whole mound of onions chopped on top and a pickle the size of a small dog. I put on my favorite baseball cap and got Carol's, and we put the sample dog on a silver tray in front of her. I fed her finely chopped hot dog a quarter of a teaspoon at a time, and I told her to look at the sample and imagine she was downing it in huge bites while watching a Red Sox game. Our friends do things like this for us. They help us see the life Jesus talked about while giving it to us in smaller pieces—sometimes just a teaspoonful at a time.

Some people have bucket lists of things they've always wanted to do. I don't have one; I want to do everything. If I had a bucket list, I could put only two or three things I *don't* want to do in it— like getting bitten in the face by a snake. But honestly, I'm even on the bubble about that one. I asked Carol if she had a bucket list of things she'd always wanted to do but had never gotten around to. Carol thought about it and then said with a twinkle in her eye, "You know, I've never toilet-papered anyone's house."

Carol called me on the walkie-talkie at four o'clock in the afternoon a few days later. "Let's go!" she almost shouted. I was going to explain to her how most toilet-papering usually happens under the cover of darkness, but then I thought about it for a sec-ond and shot back, "I'm on my way!" I got some fake rubber noses and glasses for us to put on, and we ran across the street like a couple of high school kids with rolls of toilet paper under our arms. Sweet Maria met us there and had a dozen more rolls with her. One of our favorite neighbors has some big trees in front of their home. Carol giggled as she threw rolls of toilet paper over the trees and pointed out places we'd missed. She had an arm too.

Just as we were finishing up a pretty epic job on our neighbor's trees, the police came down the street in their cruiser. It was as if they had been cued by a movie director to show up just as Carol was getting ready to heave the last roll over the top branch. She had her arm cocked behind her head as they drove up. She glanced at them, then at the tree, then back at them. They turned on their lights and started getting out of the car—and she threw it anyway. We were still wearing our disguises, so maybe she figured we could make a run for it. The policemen asked us whether we knew it was a misdemeanor to toilet-paper someone's house. I looked at them, put my arm around Carol, and said, "Officer, I've got diplomatic immunity, and she's got cancer. Go ahead and arrest us."

The officers looked at each other and grinned. They understood what was going on. They were compassionate and playful with Carol as we stood in the street talking about what prison life would be like for her. I told her she was going to love the food but hate the showers and suggested they handcuff her before they took her to the Big House just to make sure she didn't commit any other high crimes that day. We waved as the policemen drove away.

When our kids were young and had trouble sleeping, I would take the tip of my finger and rub from between their eyebrows to the end of their noses. It worked every time, and in a few minutes they'd be out cold. Carol made it through autumn to Christmas, but just barely. I would go over to her house for visits and rub Carol's nose with my finger to help her rest and escape the battle going on inside of her for a few moments. We'd pray together and talk about Jesus and our neighbors. One day, these same neighbors came to the back of her house and passed flowers they'd grown in their gardens through her window and covered Carol's bed with them. Selfless love has the power to transform even the darkest places into meadows.

When Carol had the strength, she would meet friends in her living room. She'd point out the window with a weak finger to the trees across the street with remnants of toilet paper still waving from the top branches like the flags on a circus tent. She'd giggle and say, "I did that." Throughout the winter, each day became more difficult for Carol to find energy. She slept uneasily and longer throughout the days and nights, which started to blend together for her.

On New Year's Day, Carol was clinging to life by a few threads and was far too weak to get out of bed. She'd made it to the day of the parade she had once presided over as queen. This was an ambition I think had sustained her during the last months of her courageous battle. Just before the parade started, my sons Richard and Adam, along with Lindsey's husband, Jon, went across the street and carried Carol from her bedroom to a chair they'd placed in front of her living room window facing the street.

Carol could hear the music and knew the parade was coming soon, but she couldn't see past the corner of her window. What she didn't know was that we had changed the parade route, and within a few minutes all five hundred people walked right through her front yard.

I sat next to Carol, holding her hand as hundreds of her friends and neighbors walked up to her window, pressed their noses against it, waved to her, and bounced balloons. As they did, through her tears, Carol lifted her weak hand slowly to her mouth and blew each one of them kisses goodbye. A few days later, Jesus lifted Carol up to heaven. It would be her second parade of the week.

I don't know if the streets of heaven are paved in gold, but I'm kind of hoping they're lined with balloons. And at the end of the parade, I bet we'll find Jesus blowing us kisses, rubbing our noses, and welcoming us to our next neighborhood. I just hope I get a house somewhere near Carol's again.

CHAPTER 4

The Yellow Truck

Don't tell people what they want;
tell them who they are.

When I finished law school, I bought a yellow pickup truck from my dad. It didn't have many miles on it and was in pretty good condition. I gave him the cash, he tossed me the keys, and I climbed in. As I was pulling out of the driveway, he tapped on the window and I rolled it down. He pointed at the hood and said, "You'll want to change the oil." I nodded dutifully and drove home. My dad is a great guy and I love him a lot; but it bugged me that he was still telling me what to do even though I was a grown man. However, I brushed it off as just one of those things dads do.

The next time I drove over to see my dad, we had a great visit. Before I left, he told me again how I'd want to change the oil in my truck. This seemed to happen every time we got together, and I started to see it as a kind of stalemate. I was an adult, and I didn't want someone telling me what to do. After all, this was now *my* truck. Each time my dad told me about the oil, I grumbled under my breath that I'd change the oil when I felt like it and not a minute before. Even though I knew my dad was right, I could have had five cans of Pennzoil, a funnel, and a filter in the front seat and I still wouldn't have done it.

Why? It's simple. Most people don't want to be told what they want. It's in our DNA to assess our environment, take in the inputs, and decide for ourselves what we'll do. We resist in several ways. Sometimes we send people the message with a sharp word or gesture to create some distance. Other times we resist by being passively detached and polite, while projecting a load of indifference. The reason we do this is as simple as it is complicated. Even when someone's suggestions aren't intended to be manipulative, they still feel like it.

My dad didn't mean harm when he kept telling me I should change the oil in my truck. Quite the opposite. He loved me and knew I wasn't always mindful of certain things in my life. We both knew car maintenance was one of those things. He knew that people who don't change the oil in their trucks end up with dead trucks. Because he loved me and didn't want my truck to die, he told me what I should want to do about it. He was trying to help me avoid something bad from happening, but it backfired in the way it landed with me. The same thing happens to all of us.

Some of us have been told what we want our whole lives. We've been told we should want to go out for sports or not. We should want a college education or a graduate degree or a particular career. We should want to date this person and not the other one. None of it is mean-spirited, of course, and no one means any harm. It just doesn't sit well with us.

A similar but different problem happens in our churches and schools and faith communities too. We're told by someone what God wants us to do and not do. We're told we shouldn't drink or cuss or watch certain movies. We're told we should want to have "quiet times" in the mornings and talk to strangers about "a relationship with God." We're told we should want to go on "mission trips" and "witness" to people, and sometimes we do it even if we don't really know what the words mean—but often, just for a while. After long enough, what looks like faith isn't really faith anymore. It's just compliance. The problem with mere compliance is it turns us into actors. Rather than making decisions ourselves, we read the lines off the script someone we were told to respect handed to us, and we sacrifice our ability to decide for ourselves.

The fix for all this is as easy as the problem is hard. Instead of telling people what they want, we need to tell them who they are. This works every time. We'll become in our lives whoever the people we love the most say we are.

God did this constantly in the Bible. He told Moses he was a leader and Moses became one. He told Noah he was a sailor and he became one. He told Sarah she was a mother and she became one. He told Peter he was a rock and he led the church. He told Jonah he'd be fish food and, well, he was. If we want to love people the way God loved people, let God's Spirit do the talking when it comes to telling people what they want. All the directions we're giving to each other aren't getting people to the feet of Jesus. More often, the unintended result is they lead these people back to us.

Here's the problem: when we make ourselves the hall monitor of other people's behavior, we risk having approval become more important than Jesus' love.

Another problem with trying to force compliance is it only lasts for a while, usually only until the person gets a different set of directions from someone else. Faith lasts a lifetime and will carry us through the most difficult of times without a word spoken.

Telling people what they should want turns us into a bunch of sheriffs. People who are becoming love lose the badge and give away grace instead. Tell the people you meet who they're becoming, and trust that God will help people will find their way toward beautiful things in their lives without you.

After years of driving that pickup truck, not much worked. I hadn't changed the oil in a hundred thousand miles by then. I'm not kidding. The door locks didn't work; the windshield wipers didn't work. The gas cap didn't even work. How whacked does a car need to be before the gas cap doesn't work?

I was a brand-new lawyer with a wife and a kid on the way and a job at a big law firm in San Diego. I scraped together enough money for a suit and a few shirts, but cash was tight. Parking downtown was tight too. So much so, the firm couldn't fit our cars under the building where I worked.

Each employee got two hundred dollars a month to pay for parking across the street in a fancy garage. That's a lot of money when you're broke, so I decided to keep the cash and just park my yellow truck on the street somewhere. The only place I could find was a twenty-minute walk from my office on the other side of the railroad tracks.

One winter day, I left work a little early. When I got to my truck, there was a homeless guy sitting in the driver's seat. I guess he was cold and saw the doors were unlocked, so he got in. His shopping basket was up against the passenger door on the other side. My truck was parallel parked between two other cars, and he sat there looking like he was waiting for a light to change. His hands were on the steering wheel at ten and two like they teach you in driver's education class.

I walked up to my truck and sheepishly tapped on the window. I felt like I was interrupting him. He looked up and waved at me, then stared straight ahead again, putting his hands back on the steering wheel. After a few more moments of him staring forward, I tapped on the window again. He looked up and waved. This time he rolled down my window, smiled, and asked, "Can I take you somewhere?"

"Not today," I replied as I opened the door and let him out. He swung his legs over, stood up straight next to me, crisply patted me twice on the shoulder like I was his valet, and then walked away whistling. I just stood there for a minute, my car keys still in my hand.

The next day, I drove to work in my yellow pickup truck and parked in the same place. At the end of the day, I came back to my truck and there he was again. I tapped on the window, he waved at me, and I waved back. He asked if he could take me somewhere, I said no, and he opened the door. He stretched, and we swapped places again. This went on for months. We didn't talk much during any of these exchanges. It was kind of like the changing of the guard at Buckingham Palace but without the fur hats. He needed a place to stay, and I needed an oil change. People in need find each other.

What this man really needed was a secure place to spend his days. Someplace warm and dry. What I really needed was to feel like I was being helpful. We both were doing something about it. I never got his name and he didn't get mine. I didn't know what he did, and he didn't know I was a lawyer. I didn't know why he was homeless or for how long, and he didn't know I hadn't changed the oil. I just knew I looked forward to seeing him at the end of each day and I think he liked seeing me. We had found our rhythm together and didn't need all the other details.

One day I came back to my truck after work, and from a block away I could see my friend wasn't sitting in the driver's seat. That was strange. I was kind of sad to see he wasn't there and wondered what had happened as I walked closer. When I got to the truck I found out why. My truck was trashed. There were empty beer bottles, half-smoked cigarettes, and garbage on the floor. A couple of knobs on the dashboard were gone. It was a mess. I knew why he wasn't there. He was ashamed.

Shame does that to us. It makes us leave safe places. It breaks the rhythms we've established with each other. This guy and I had never needed words. After he made a mistake that day, he no doubt thought there would be many words he'd need to give me, but shame makes us silent. It strips us of the few words we might have. It mutes our life and our love. It's the pickpocket of our confidence.

I hadn't done much for him. We hadn't had any real conversations in the many months we'd known each other. I treated him with the same quiet respect he treated me with. We just traded places once a day. Evidently, that day something had gone terribly wrong and he didn't know what to do, so he left and I never saw him again.

We can't allow this to happen between us. Shame will do this, and fears will too. Dumb arguments will do it. Pride and its unreasonable expectations will do it. Our failures and embarrassment will do it. Each of these will tell us as many lies as we'll listen to, then steal our words, rob us of the rhythms we've established with people we've come to know, and tell us to run away.

I drove that yellow pickup truck for 120,000 miles—and do you know what? I never changed the oil. Not even once. This, of course, did irreparable damage to the engine. I drove down the street each day with white smoke billowing out of the exhaust pipe. I looked like Uncle Buck. Most of us will do almost anything, even foolish things, to avoid being told what it is we want. When someone tries to control us, it teaches us new ways to be dumb because it reminds us of old ways we've been manipulated before.

One morning, I walked out of my house to get in my yellow truck, but it wasn't there. I wondered for a second as I walked back inside the house with my keys whether I'd loaned the truck to someone. Did I forget it downtown? Was my friend sitting in it somewhere with his hands at ten and two? Nope. Someone had stolen it. It wouldn't be hard to do. There were no locks. The stolen truck wouldn't be hard to find either. The police could just follow the trail of white smoke.

A couple of weeks later, the police called and said they'd found the truck. But I didn't want it anymore. It barely ran. With a bit of distance, I realized for the first time how messed up it really was and how correct my father had been years earlier.

Jesus told His friends a story about a father and a lost son. The boy wasn't spending his days in the driver's seats of other people's trucks, but pretty close. He'd messed up and felt really bad about what he'd done, just like my friend by the railroad tracks did. But when he was found, something different happened to the son than to my yellow-truck friend. The son ran back toward the relationship he had with his father, not away from it. It's something we all get to decide whether we'll do. You've probably messed up a couple of times. Me too. Run back toward God, not away from Him.

The father in Jesus' story ran toward the son too. When the father found out the son wasn't lost anymore, he celebrated in ways I couldn't when I found my trashed truck. I think I know why. There was no shame. The father wasn't thinking about how badly the son had messed up. The son wasn't thinking about it either. They both knew the son had steered his life right off a cliff, but somehow they got past the shame of the failure and got to the celebration of being together once again.

Do lots of that. Find your way back to the people you've loved and who have loved you. Figure out who you've broken your rhythm with. Don't let the misunderstanding decide your future. If you lost your way with God, let Him close the distance between

you and start the celebration again. We're all in the same truck when it comes to our need for love and acceptance and forgiveness.

What made sense to me when I first heard about Jesus is how He doesn't give us a bunch of directions intended to manipulate our behavior or control our conduct. Instead, He has beautiful hopes for us and has told us what those are, but He isn't scowling at us when we're not yet ready to have those same hopes for ourselves. He won't love us more or less based on how we act, and He's more interested in our hearts than all the things we do. He's not stuck telling us what to do, when to do it, or what we want either. Far better, He continues to tell us through our successes and our mistakes who we are, and here's what He wants us to know—we are His.

CHAPTER 5

Limo Driver

Don't build a castle when you
can build a kingdom.

I received a call from someone organizing a national conference for Christian radio broadcasters. He said they meet once a year and their next meeting would be at Disney World in Orlando. They wanted me to speak at the event, and he asked me to pray about whether I should come.

"You pray about it," I told him. "It's Disney World. I'm coming!"

I don't know if just thinking about something is the same as praying about something. Probably not. I think people often get the two confused. Prayers sometimes are spontaneous cries out to God for help and other times are well-organized attempts to lift our voices together for a specific purpose. I've never related to scripted prayers. It would be like my kids talking to me, or Jesus talking to His friends, using 3x5-inch note cards. When I do it right, my prayers feel like a conversation with a friend and my words feel more like breaths of air than fancy speeches. We need every type of prayer I suppose, but I don't think we need to sound like each other. God isn't wowed by fancy words; He delights in humble hearts.

I couldn't wait to get to the radio broadcasters event so I could see what Disney World in Florida looked like. I'm a yellow cab guy, so I got off the plane in Orlando and walked over to the taxi stand. On the way there, I saw a guy with a black hat, a suit, and a sign standing in front of a long black limo. His sign had "Bob" written on it. My first thought was he was there to pick up another guy named Bob. Maybe Bob Dylan was in town? I'd always wanted to meet him. Then I noticed "Goff" under the name on the sign. My instinct was to walk right past the limo guy. But then I thought, *What the heck. I've never been in a limo before. If they spent the cash to rent one, I'm going for a ride!*

I walked up to the guy with the hat and the sign and said in my loudest and most enthusiastic outdoor voice, "I'm Bob!" I waved my arms like I usually do when I'm talking to people I don't know. He looked me up and down for a second and then asked, "Yes, but *who are you?*" He wanted to know if I was famous, I suppose. I wanted to tell him, "Yes, I invented medicine," but simply said, "I'm just Bob." He looked more than a little disappointed.

"I know, man. Me too," I said.

I got in the back of the limo, and we started driving toward the Magic Kingdom. I know God lives everywhere, but I bet He spends a lot of time at Disney World. It's a place where no one uses big words and what anyone does for a day job doesn't matter. It's a place without titles and status and where no one is stuck being who they were, unless they want to be. It's where our imaginations get permission to go on all the rides and our fears aren't allowed to take cuts in front of us anymore.

I have the architectural plans for the castle at Disneyland. They came up for sale on eBay. I couldn't believe it. I bid my wife's car for them. She walks around town a lot now. Building a castle isn't as hard as you'd think if you've got enough time, space, and cash. Just get a lot of plywood, pixie dust, and a bunch of people swinging hammers and putting drawbridges in place, and you'll have one after a while.

We actually build castles all the time, out of our jobs and our families and the things we've purchased. Sometimes we even make them out of each other. Some of these castles are impressive too. Lots of people come to admire what we've built over the course of our lives and tell us what great castles we have. But Jesus told His friends we weren't supposed to spend our lives building castles. He said He wanted us to build a kingdom, and there's a big difference between building a castle and building a kingdom.

You see, castles have moats to keep creepy people out, but kingdoms have bridges to let everyone in. Castles have dungeons for people who have messed up, but kingdoms have grace. There's one last thing castles have—trolls. You've probably met a couple. I have too. Trolls aren't bad people; they're just people I don't really understand. Here's the deal: it's how we treat the trolls in our lives that will let us know how far along we are in our faith. If we want a kingdom, then we start the way grace did, by drawing a circle around everyone and saying they're in. Kingdoms are built from the people up. There's no set of plans—just Jesus.

There are plenty of people I don't understand. I suppose some are trolls and some aren't. God doesn't see people the way I do, though. The ones I see as problems, God sees as sons and daughters, made in His image. The ones I see as difficult, He sees as delightfully different. The fact is, what skews my view of people who are sometimes hard to be around is that God is working on different things in their lives than He is working on in mine. I'll give you an example. There's a story in the Bible about Jesus and His friends going across a lake where they met a guy who was a troll to most of the people near him. He was mean, crazy, possessed. Jesus knew exactly what was going on in him even when the people who lived nearby didn't. You may know what happened. All the evil in him left and went into the pigs, and the pigs ran off a cliff and died. What was a great day for the guy Jesus met was an equally lousy day for a pig farmer nearby and was even a worse day for the pigs.

I can almost hear the conversation the farmer must have had that night when his wife asked how his day at work was. "Well, it was going great," the guy probably continued, "until a guy landed his boat on the shore and started talking to the crazy guy by the lake." After a pause, he said, shaking his head, "Then all two thousand of our pigs ran off a cliff and died."

"What? How come?" his wife must have asked. The simple answer is, he probably didn't know. The real answer was that God was doing something different in someone else's life than he was in their lives, and what He was doing intersected the pig farmer's life in a big way.

God knows we're easily confused and often wayward, and He pursues us with love anyway. I think He wants us to see things the way He does, and it's not going to happen from the top floor of our castles. It will happen at the ground level of grace. And it's going to take a lot of grace to accept that sometimes we're the person on the other side of the lake, and other times we're the pig farmer.

God wants me to love the ones I don't understand, to get to know their names. To invite them to do things with me. To go and find the ones everyone has shunned and turned away. To see them as my neighbors even if we are in totally different places. You'll be able to spot people who are becoming love because they want to build kingdoms, not castles. They fill their lives with people who don't look like them or act like them or even believe the same things as them. They treat them with love and respect and are more eager to learn from them than presume they have something to teach.

There's a tradition at Disney most people don't know about. The windows in the second-story shops are dedicated to people who helped build the kingdom there. At Disneyland in Southern California, I found a window across from the Jungle Cruise for a guy named Harper Goff. He's not related to me at all, but that's not what I tell the people who sell tickets to get in. The window says,

"Prof. Harper Goff—Banjo Lessons." But banjo isn't what he'll be remembered for. You see, Harper Goff has a window at Disneyland because he helped build a kingdom there.

Here's the question I keep asking myself: *What do I want my window to say?* This question is worth thinking about even if you don't know the answer. What part are you going to play in building the kind of kingdom Jesus said would outlast us all?

We have a lodge up in Canada. It's a tradition we've had for decades that everyone who comes to visit us climbs under the dining room table to sign it and leave a word behind. One of my friends, Don, left the word *With* on the bottom of the table. We've had leaders and ambassadors and ministers of foreign affairs and elementary school kids sign under our table and leave a word. We've had good guys and bad guys and undecided do the same. We've had rockers and poets and Supreme Court justices and moviemakers climb under the table. We've had people whose countries were rolling tanks against each other climb under together with pens and leave their words. One of the many reasons Don has been so influential in my life is that he taught me the importance of being "with" each other.

I don't know what God would put on His table if He had one. I don't think He'd want to have it read like a poem or look like a painting. I think He would just want it to say "With." He wouldn't need a twenty-dollar phrase or a thirty-word Bible verse. He demonstrated the word *with* is much bigger and worthier and more accessible than any ten Bible verses. It also doesn't rhyme with anything, which is a plus. It doesn't sound like a big theological statement, because it's not. It's a huge theological statement. It's God's purpose for us. It's the reason Jesus came. It's the whole Bible in a word. People who are becoming love are *with* those who are hurting and help them get home. I've always thought that people who didn't want to be with people here are going to hate heaven. Truly, it will be everybody, always there.

I got into the back of the limo and talked to the driver through the window dividing us as we traversed Orlando on the highway. The driver was a friendly, engaging guy. After we'd driven a short time, I said, "You know, this is the first time I've ever been to Orlando, but if someone asked me what I thought about everyone in the city, you know what I'd tell them? I'd say I think everyone in Orlando is just terrific. Do you know why? It's simple—because you're a nice guy!"

I thought how the opposite was true as well. If the limo driver had been mean or rude or pushy with me and someone asked me what I thought of everyone in Orlando, I would have said, "I think everyone in Orlando is mean or rude or pushy." Neither statement would be true, but somehow, because of how we're wired, when we've met one person we feel as if we've met everybody.

Think about it. If you know just one person in Mexico or the Philippines or Bolivia or Lichtenstein and something happens in one of those countries, don't you feel a kinship with everyone there? It feels like we've met everybody in those countries even though, obviously, we haven't yet.

I bet this is what Jesus meant when He told His friends that people would understand who He was by watching how we treated each other. Early on I thought big acts of generosity or great sermons or arenas full of people singing songs would help us understand God's love for us. He said it was none of these. Jesus told His friends that letting people see the way we love each other would be the best way to let people know about Him. It wouldn't be because we'd given them a lot of directions or instructions or because they memorized or studied all the right things. It would be because someone met you or me and felt as if they'd just met Jesus. I think what He meant was He wanted someone to meet a person who loved Him and then feel like they had just met heaven— everyone there.

We drove a little farther through the city, and the driver told me about his life and the people he loved. He also said he'd been driving limos for twenty-five years. "Wow," I said. "I bet you've met some interesting people in that time—not me, of course, but you know, famous people."

"I have," he said. "I'm really going to miss this job, because I'm retiring next month."

I sat back in my seat, watched the palm trees pass by for a few more minutes, and then I had a thought. I leaned forward and said through the glass, "Hey buddy, have you ever ridden in the back of one of these limos? I bet you'd love it. They're terrific!"

He laughed and said, "Of course not. I'd get fired."

Now I had my arm through the glass between the driver's seat and the living-room-sized back seats in the limo. I think I even got a shoulder through the window. "Hey, you're retiring anyway. Pull over!" I said.

And you know what?

He did!

I got out of the back of the car, and we swapped places. He got in the back, and I put on his hat and jumped behind the wheel and drove us to Disney World. He got there about fifteen minutes after me—it was a pretty long limo.

I carry medals with me all the time. They don't say anything on them. I'm a lawyer, so the medals mean whatever I say they mean. I opened the door and let my limo-driver friend out from the back seat. He stood up and straightened his jacket, and I was still wearing his hat. I pinned a medal on his chest and said, "You're brave. You're courageous. You're foolhardy! Did you see how I took that last turn?" I spoke words of truth and affirmation to him with a smile. I patted him on the chest, gave him a hug, and walked into the hotel.

When the limo driver went home that night to the woman he's been living with for the past ten years, do you think he told her he'd met a Christian guy that day who told him he was supposed to be married? Of course not! I bet he told her he'd met a guy who told him who he was.

That's our job. It's always been our job. We're supposed to just love the people in front of us. We're the ones who tell them who they are. We don't need to spend as much time as we do telling people what we think about what they're doing. Loving people doesn't mean we need to control their conduct. There's a big difference between the two. Loving people means caring without an agenda. As soon as we have an agenda, it's not love anymore. It's acting like you care to get someone to do what you want or what you think God wants them to do. Do less of that, and people will see a lot less of you and more of Jesus.

Talk behind each other's backs constantly. Just talk about the right stuff. Talk about Jesus. Talk about grace. Talk about love and acceptance. People don't grow where they are informed; they grow where they're loved and accepted. Talk about who people are becoming and who you see them turning into. And give people medals, lots of them. The people around us should be walking around looking like the chairman of the Joint Chiefs of Staff. They should jingle when they walk.

It's this simple: I want people to meet you and me and feel like they've just met everyone in heaven.

CHAPTER 6

Skydiving

God was with us so we'd be with each other.

My son Adam is out of college and is fearless. He'll try anything once, but he'll do it several times if it's life-threatening. If you can't lose your arm doing it, he's usually not interested. He started taking skydiving lessons this year. These weren't the tandem jumps I was familiar with, where an experienced skydiving instructor is attached to the novice. These were solo jumps.

Understandably, there's quite a bit of on-the-ground training involved in getting a skydiving license. In addition to taking some pretty involved classes before you get in the airplane, there are quite a few solo jumps you need to make with an instructor free-falling nearby to make sure you don't freak out and crater. While there's more instruction than I thought, there certainly isn't as much as is needed.

When the kids were growing up, we weren't a family you

would find at the local field every weekend for Little League baseball or soccer. I would have had our children join a team just so I could eat the corn dogs, but the kids never seemed interested in organized sports, so we skipped most of it. Going out to the drop zone each weekend to watch Adam skydive felt a little like what I imagined going to a Little League game would be like. Except my son, the shortstop, would be falling from thirteen thousand feet. An unforced error in skydiving would be more of a game changer than a ball going between his legs near second base. This was more than a little unsettling to me as I watched him strap on his parachute each weekend, get in a plane with no door on it, and fly away.

Squinting as I looked toward the sun to find the airplane two miles overhead, I watched as Adam jumped out and started his free fall. He was smaller than an ant silhouetted against the bright blue sky. The free fall looks pretty slow from below, but the skydiver is actually falling through the air at two hundred fifty feet per second. Between the time Adam jumped out of the plane and the time the parachute opened, he had free-fallen a distance greater than twenty one-hundred-story buildings stacked end to end. That's a lot of down elevator. Adam explained to me with a wink that all he needs to do to get the parachute to deploy is to reach behind him while he's falling at 140 mph and find a small hacky sack ball connected to the main parachute to throw out. I always imagined if it were me doing the reaching, it wouldn't be a hacky sack I'd find.

If the main parachute comes out, it gives a huge tug as it snaps full of air. If it doesn't, I suppose it would look just like zooming in on Google Earth really fast. I know how forgetful

Adam can sometimes be, so as he fell I found myself shouting from below, "Pull the chute! Pull the chute! Pull the chute!" and reaching behind myself as I did. After what always seemed like way too long, I would see the parachute open and hear Adam yelping with excitement and gliding in figure eights back to the grass field near the runway.

Some people listen to Christmas carols only in December, but I listen to them all the time. They also read the Christmas story only once a year. I read it every couple of months. It tells us God said, "The virgin will conceive and give birth to a son, and they will call him *Immanuel*." A couple of verses later it says they "gave him the name *Jesus* . . ." At first, I wondered if perhaps Mary had twins.

Immanuel means "God with us." As a father, I know what it feels like to want to be with your children. When God sent Jesus into the world, He demonstrated He didn't just want to be an observer in the lives of the ones He loved. He wanted to be a participant. He wanted to be *with* the ones He loved. I do too.

After months of taking Adam to the drop zone each weekend, I decided to blow Adam's mind. So while he was at work one week, I took skydiving lessons.

When I dropped Adam off the following week, he got out of the car, put on his parachute, buckled his straps, and got into the airplane. It was time for my big reveal, so I got out of the car, threw a parachute over my shoulders, buckled the straps, and got in the plane too. Adam did a double take as I sat down next to him.

"Dad, what are you doing?" Adam asked in disbelief.

"How hard could it be?" I shot back with a wink as I adjusted my helmet.

The plane started its engines, and we rolled down the runway. When Adam and I were a few miles up in the air, the plane engines slowed a bit, the pilot turned on a green light to let us know we were over the field, and we moved to the door. There are plenty of things to do to get ready to skydive, like pack your parachute, make a will, and say goodbye to loved ones. Once you get in the door to jump, there are only three things to remember: up, down, and out. That's it. You practice this on the ground several times before you get in the plane. You rock up on your toes to let the people around you know you're about to go, you crouch down like you're about to jump, and then it's right out the door.

You exit the plane into a 100-mph wind and immediately disappear from view. When Adam got to the door, he yelled, "See you on the ground!" He rocked up, down, and jumped out. Not surprisingly, Adam did a backflip as he jumped out the door and disappeared from view. I'm not really sure what came over me in the moment, but there was a massive jolt of adrenaline and an overwhelming desire to be *with* Adam in the air as he fell.

I sprang to the door, blew off all the up, down, and out stuff, and threw myself out of the plane with everything I had. I jumped so hard, I jumped right out of my tennis shoes. No joke. Try doing that sometime. It's not easy, but it's what it looks like to want to be *with* someone that bad.

I was free-falling in my socks and laughed when I realized what I'd done. After a long minute of free-falling, I reached behind me and pulled on the hacky sack, the parachute came out, and I landed in a field near Adam. He pretended he didn't know me as I walked in my socks over to the airplane after it landed to get my tennis shoes back.

I know a little bit more now what it feels like to be a father who wants to be *with* his kids. Jesus did something a lot like what I did with Adam. He jumped out of heaven to be with us.

I have been watching Adam for his whole life. I know all about Adam, and he knows quite a bit about me. Still, there's a big difference between knowing what someone's doing and being *with* them while they do it. God knew we'd know the difference too. This has been the easiest way for me to understand one reason that God sent Jesus to us. He wasn't sent because God was mad at us. He jumped out of heaven and came as Immanuel because He wanted to be God *with* us.

I've taken plenty of bar exams in the course of my career as a lawyer and have been licensed to practice law in quite a few states. Each of these bar exams takes between two and three days depending on the state, and they test everything you know about the law. By the end, your mind feels like melted Velveeta because you've gone through more than thirty long hours of testing. Guess how long the final test is while you're free-falling to get your skydiving license? Half a minute. No lie. All you have to do is simply obey what you're told to do for just thirty seconds.

Some people I've met who like Jesus a lot have told me they're going to do whatever He tells them to do for the rest of their lives. I think that's terrific. While I'd like to say the same thing with even half the confidence they have, I just can't. It's easy to talk about big ambitions you have for your faith, and theirs is certainly a beautiful one. I've started a couple of diets this way on January first, but I didn't make it as far as I thought I would. What I've been doing with my faith is this: instead of saying I'm going to *believe* in Jesus for my whole life, I've been trying to actually *obey* Jesus for thirty seconds at a time.

Here's how it works: When I meet someone who is hard to get along with, I think, *Can I love that person for the next thirty seconds?* While they continue to irritate me, I find myself counting silently, . . . *twenty-seven, twenty-eight, twenty-nine* . . . and before I get to thirty, I say to myself, *Okay, I'm going to love that person for thirty more seconds.* This is what I've been doing with the difficult commands of Jesus too. Instead of agreeing with all of them, I'm trying to obey God for thirty seconds at a time and live into them. I try to love the person in front of me the way Jesus did for the next thirty seconds rather than merely agree with Jesus and avoid them entirely, which I'm sad to say comes easier to me. I try to see difficult people in front of me for who they could become some-day, and I keep reminding myself about this possibility for thirty seconds at a time.

It's easy to agree with what Jesus said. What's hard is actually doing what Jesus did. For me, agreeing is cheap and obeying is costly. Obeying is costly because it's uncomfortable. It makes me grow one decision and one discussion at a time. It makes me put away my pride. These are the kinds of decisions that aren't made once for a lifetime; they're made thirty seconds at a time.

When you're getting your skydiving license, most of the class isn't spent talking about what happens when things go right and the parachute opens correctly. Instead, they prepare you for what to do when it doesn't. That seemed like a good idea to me. One of the things they teach you feels counterintuitive. The parachute is connected to your harness by hundreds of small strings. When it opens, you're supposed to look up and see if all the strings are where they're supposed to be. If there is just one string caught over the top of the parachute, they tell you to cut away the entire parachute, start free-falling again, then pull the emergency chute. I remember thinking, *Are you kidding me? There's no way I'm cutting away an almost perfect parachute because one small string out of hundreds of them is out of place. It's good enough, right?* Here's the problem. If even one string is over the top, then the parachute will look like it's fine while you're up in the air, but you'll never be able to land it. You won't realize this until you get close to the ground and hit hard. The same is true with our lives.

I've tried to fly my faith more than a couple of times with a few strings over the top. Maybe you have too. It was colorful and looked good on the outside. To most people, it even appeared to be flying the way it was supposed to. I wasn't trying to fake it or be a fraud. Most of us aren't. While I knew I had a string or two over the top, the idea of cutting away everything and starting all over again sounded excessive to me. It sounded reckless, unsafe. Perhaps it does to you too. It didn't to Jesus, though. He said He wanted us to become new creations. His plan for our renewal is that we cut away all the things hanging us up and start all over again each day with Him. He talked about cutting away things that entangle us and about pruning more than parachutes, but the concept is the same. When we get the wrong things over the top of our lives, we might look good for a short time, but we won't land our lives well. If you have a string or two over the top of your life, cut it away. Will it be scary? You bet. Do it anyway.

There's one last thing the instructor told us in class. He said if the main parachute doesn't open up, and the reserve parachute doesn't either, you've got about forty-five seconds before you hit the ground and make your mark. I was surprised and a little grossed out when the instructor said hitting the ground isn't what kills you. Every bone in your body will break, of course. But after you hit the ground, you'll bounce—and it's the second time you hit that kills you as the broken bones puncture all your organs. I know that is kind of graphic, but it's true.

I'm a lawyer, so with this information in mind I figured I needed a strategy. Here's mine: if none of the parachutes open up, when I hit the ground, I'm going to grab the grass and avoid the bounce. What is true in skydiving is true in our lives. It's usually not the initial failure that takes any of us out; it's the bounce. We've all hit the ground hard at work or in a relationship or with a big ambition. Whether we had a big, public failure or an even bigger private one, the initial failure won't crush our spirit or kill our faith; it's the second hit that does. The second hit is what follows when things go massively wrong or we fail big, and the people we thought would rush to us create distance instead. They express disapproval or treat us with polite indifference.

If we want to be like Jesus, here's our simple and courageous job: Catch people on the bounce. When they mess up, reach out to them with love and acceptance the way Jesus did. When they hit hard, run to them with your arms wide open to hug them even harder. God wants to be *with* them when they mess up, and He wants us to participate.

I keep putting on my parachute and getting in the plane with Adam on the weekends. Truth be known, I don't like skydiving as much as he does, but I like Adam a lot. Find what the people you love want to do and then go be with them in it. If Adam wanted to make pizzas, I'd grow the tomatoes. Be with each other. Don't just gather information about people who have failed big or are in need—go be *with* them. When you get there, don't just be in proximity—be present. Catch them. Don't try to teach them. There's a big difference.

We don't need a plan to do these things. We don't need to wait for just the right moment. We just need to show up, grab a parachute, and when it's time, jump out of our shoes after people the way Jesus jumped out of heaven to be with us.

Sometimes we make loving people a lot more complicated than Jesus did. We don't need to anymore. It's just up, down, and out.

CHAPTER 7

A Day at the Museum

It doesn't matter what our faith looks
like; it matters what it is.

Have you ever been to Madame Tussauds? It's a wax museum. It's where all bees go to retire. There are several of these museums around the world, and I've been to them all. Sometimes I ask the person selling tickets where I can find a candlewick and some matches just to see the response. But I'm not fascinated with the wax people. I love looking at the real people who go to wax museums to look at wax people. Do it sometime. Honest. It's worth the price of admission.

Everyone's there: Abraham Lincoln, George Washington, Elvis. It's like a reunion of the dead. If I were in charge of the wax museum, I'd have an exhibit of a wax person with way too much body hair, waxing themselves. Nobody would get it, of course, but I'd still think it was pretty funny.

I was in Washington, DC, awhile back for some meetings. I

had on a black suit, a trench coat, and my best clip-on tie. With my white hair and whiskers, I looked just like a senator. I had the kids with me and could tell they were a little bored, so I asked them, "Hey, do you want to go to the wax museum?" They'd never gone, so they jumped at the chance. We got to Madame Tussauds and ran downstairs to where all the wax people were. When we got there, just for fun, I struck a pose between the third and fourth wax guys on display. I whispered to the kids, "Watch this." They all shook their heads, saying, "Dad, would you please act your age?" I put my finger to my lips and whispered, "I am."

I could hear a couple of people coming, so I froze. Two little old ladies were heading my way. When they came around the corner, they walked up to me and got uncomfortably close to my face. One of the elderly women licked her finger and touched my cheek. I thought I might hurl, but I didn't. The other reached out her hand and pulled on my whiskers with her pinched fingers. They looked at each other in amazement and then back at me again and said, "He looks so real."

Because I'm a lawyer, I knew I couldn't move. I was almost certain one, or both of them, would have strokes and someone would end up owning my house. So I froze and took it like a wax man. After a long minute or two, they moved on to the next wax guy and began pinching his face and pulling on his clothing. When they were a safe distance away, I caught the corner of their eyes as they looked back. I took a step forward, waved at them, and mouthed the words, "I'm not wax." One of the ladies dropped her handbag and froze. Meanwhile, Lindsey, Richard, and Adam were bolting for the exit to hail a cab for a fast getaway.

Do you know what I realized about myself that day? I'm a really good poser. It's probably why I'm a pretty good lawyer. You see, I know how to fake it really well. You probably do too. Most of us have been posers at one time or another, if we're honest. People who are becoming love stop faking it about who they are and where they are in their lives and their faith.

When I was in high school, there was a trick if someone who was eighteen wanted to pass for someone who was twenty-one. If their birth year ended with a 9, they could take their driver's license, razorblade out the 9, flip it over, and glue it back in as a 6. This inversion made it appear on the license that they were three years older than they were. It was a felony and it could land them in jail, but they could instantly gain three years in age.

Licenses are a little more sophisticated now than they were then. Still, a lot of people are cutting out parts of their life, flipping them over, and pretending to be someone they aren't yet. We all do it to greater or lesser degrees. It's not for malicious reasons. We all have this idea of who we want to be, so while we're getting there, it's easy to pretend we're older or smarter or even believe in God more than we actually do. The longer we've been doing it, the better we get at it, or so it seems. God, of course, sees right through it, and quite often the people around us do too. The sad fact is, we're usually the only ones getting fooled.

We get so good at fooling other people and reading our own news clippings about who we are that we end up believing we've arrived at a place we haven't yet. It's why some of us buy expensive cars or boats or homes we can't really afford. We've fooled ourselves into thinking we can afford it now, when we won't actually be able to afford it for a few years. It's why we take leadership positions or get on stages when we're still working out the basics in our own faith. It's like we've flipped the 9 and made it a 6. But God sees right through the things we forge in our lives.

There was a guy and his wife in the Bible named Ananias and Sapphira who sold some property. They lived in a community where everyone's needs were being met and they wanted to do their part, so they sold their land. When I first read this story, I was blown away at the generosity of these two. I haven't met anyone who sold a home or a plot of land and dropped off the money at the local church or community center. A lawnmower, a couple of used books, an outdated laptop, or an old mattress, maybe, but all the money from selling their land? I've never heard of anything even close.

There's a hill behind our house in San Diego. Sweet Maria tells me to hike it to get some exercise. I'm good for about three round trips up and down before I'm worn out. One week, I wanted to impress her and prove what great shape I was in. I told her all week how I was going to hike the hill five times on Saturday. I told her on Monday and Tuesday, "I'm going up that hill five times next weekend!" I told her the same thing on Wednesday and Thursday: "I'm going up that hill five times next weekend." I told her the same thing on Friday: "I'm going up that hill five times!" Saturday morning finally came. I laced up my shoes and headed for the hill. When I got back, Sweet Maria asked me how many times I'd gone up the hill. I puffed out my chest and with five outstretched fingers said in my most manly voice, "I went up that hill five times!"

Then I thought about it for a second.

I'd only gone up the hill three times, just like always.

I wasn't trying to fib or mislead anyone. What happened was simply this: I'd told myself I was going to go up that hill five times on Saturday so many times I actually believed I'd done it.

The same thing happens in our faith. We hope for good things to happen to people in need. We hope it and we hope it and we hope it some more. When we do, our brain can fool us into thinking we're actually helping. But hoping isn't helping. Hoping is just hoping. Don't be fooled. It's easy to do.

Ananias and Sapphira loved God a lot. They sold their land and gave all the money away—well, almost all of it. I bet on Monday and Tuesday Ananias told God and everyone around him he was going to sell his land and give it all away. He probably said the same thing on Wednesday and Thursday: "I'm giving it all away." He probably told everybody on Friday the same thing again: "I'm giving it all away." On Saturday morning, he came to his friends and they asked how much was there. Ananias proudly said, "All of it!" You might remember how the story went. He had kept some of the money for himself and his wife. It was an entirely reasonable thing to do. I do it all the time. It didn't go well for them.

Ananias was posing as someone he wasn't yet, and he and his wife both dropped dead. It sounds more than a little harsh. We throw a couple of one-dollar bills wrapped in a twenty in the offering plate and feel great. We donate a little to a charity and get a wristband or throw a few bucks at a Kickstarter campaign and get an album or a hoodie. We feel terrific. Even if Ananias and Sapphira gave away only a quarter of the money they got from selling their land, I bet they would have bested my most generous year. So why did they drop dead?

I don't think anyone knows for sure. My best guess, though, is God saw they were posing and wasn't happy about it. They were saying to everyone around them that they were at a place they hadn't arrived at yet. They probably wanted to be the people who would give it all away. They weren't trying to fool everyone. They had probably said what they hoped to do so often they actually thought they had done it. The fact was, they just weren't there yet. Me neither. It's the problem posers like all of us have.

Chilling words followed from a man named Peter, whom they had given the money to—"You have not lied just to human beings but to God." We all do that a lot more than we'd like to admit. Every time we try to pass ourselves off in front of people like we're at a different place than we really are, we end up back at the wax museum.

I don't think God's in the business of striking people dead who misrepresent where they are with Him. If He were, who would be left standing? The story about Ananias lets us know, however, just how strongly God feels about us keeping it real and transparent and honest about where we actually are, rather than faking it and pretending we're someone we only hope to be someday. I think God can use us wherever we are. The Bible is full of stories of people who messed up. It seems like failure in the world was a requirement for success with God. People who are becoming love keep it real about who they are right now, while living in constant anticipation about who God's helping them become.

When they make movies in Hollywood, the director will have an assistant with a black-and-white clapperboard stand in front of the actor and make a noise when the cameras start rolling. This gives a marker for the moviemaker to sync the audio and video later. We've all seen bad movies where the audio track isn't quite synced up with the video track. What you hear isn't aligned with what you see people saying. It's usually not a big difference, but it can become a big distraction.

My son Richard is an amazingly talented and creative guy. He makes videos like a boss and was helping me with one of mine. We didn't have a clapperboard when we were filming, so Richard just had me clap my hands to make the marker for syncing up the audio and video. These days, when I'm speaking to a group of people and find myself talking about the man I wish I was, rather than the person I am right now, I clap my hands to remind myself to sync up what I'm saying with what I'm doing.

We should all have beautiful ambitions for our lives and who we might become, but we also need to sync it up so we're not fooled into believing we've already arrived at a place in our faith we've only been thinking about going to someday.

Have you noticed when people take photographs of each other, the person taking the picture is usually smiling too? Check it out for yourself. I think God does the same thing when He sees us. He's not trying to bust us when we fail or when we act like posers. He doesn't hang photographs of our mess-ups on the refrigerator. God isn't in the business of punishing us with reminders; instead, He pursues us with love. He doesn't grimace at our failures; He delights in our attempts.

Here's the deal: when we act like someone we're not, it's often because we're not happy with who we are. We might think we need other people's permission or love or approval before we can live our lives and pursue our beautiful ambitions. It's both good and bad. It's good if it causes us to want to pursue Jesus' love and approval more. But it's bad if we miss out on who God uniquely made us to be so we can be who someone else thinks we should be. God has never looked in your mirror or mine and wished He saw someone else.

Every time we fake it and aren't authentic, we make God's love for us look fake too. He doesn't have a wax figure of us somewhere that looks smarter or taller or shorter or skinnier or more ripped than us. He doesn't want us to just look different. He wants us to become love. It won't be because we talked about who we wished we were over and over again or because we gave ourselves enough positive affirmations in the mirror. Only love has the power to get us there.

God isn't shaking His head in disapproval as we make our way toward Him. He's got His arms outstretched, welcoming us home to Him with love. I bet if we could hear what He's thinking, we'd hear Him whispering, "You've got this. Just keep moving toward Me."

Do you want to do something amazing for God? Trade the appearance of being close to God for the power of actually being close to God. Quit talking a big game and go live a big faith. One of Jesus' friends said if we want to get it right, we need to live a life worthy of the calling we've received. The call is to love God and the people around us while we live into the most authentic version of ourselves. We weren't just an idea God hoped would work out someday. We were one of His most creative expressions of love, ever.

Lose the wax. Don't fake it; sync it up. Go be you.

CHAPTER 8

The Pizza Place

What we've spent our time collecting
might not be worth it.

There's a pizza place near our house. I love this place—kind of. They make noise there. Lots of it. I'm certain it's where all the noise in the universe is manufactured. I suspect they have machines in the back rooms filled with vats of the stuff. I bet it gets dropped off in the middle of the night after junior high school basketball games where noise is collected by the barrel. NASA probably sends its astronauts to this place to prepare them for the deafening noise of rocket launches. My best guess is that the noise they don't pipe into their pizza parlors they sell to heavy metal bands for the guys to lip-sync to. The rest is released into the atmosphere. It's actually what is melting all of our ice caps.

Each of the stores in the pizza chain runs on pure sugar, but they also serve pizza. Lots of pizza. Some people think it tastes like dog food, but I like it. One thing I don't get—their mascot is an animal we used to set traps for around the house. What marketing guy thinks up this stuff? To me, this looks like one big class-action lawsuit waiting to happen.

There are also lots of games. Some of these games give the players tickets when they play them. I think it's why everyone puts up with all the noise and pizza they don't like. They've figured out people will do just about anything for a handful of tickets. One game was always a favorite for our kids. It's called Skee-Ball. It's like a miniature bowling alley got together with a skateboard ramp. There are holes at the far end that always appear to be just smaller than the balls you roll at them. If one of the balls does get in a hole, which happens infrequently, lights flash and a few red tickets roll out of the game. You can cash in these tickets for prizes at a booth near the door if you want to.

I'd been taking my kids to this pizza place for years, and we'd spend most of our time playing Skee-Ball. We got pretty good at it. Only a few of the balls I rolled flew through nearby store windows. We saved up all our tickets in a shoebox for a long time so we could trade them in someday and get something really terrific. Finally, after years of collecting tickets, I went to the prize counter with my box of tickets. I bet I had a thousand of them. I thought I was going to get a Porsche. I shoved the red tickets across the counter like they were salmon and I was the captain of a big Alaskan fishing boat.

The guy behind the counter counted my tickets once and recounted them to make sure he got it right. When he was all done, you know what they gave me? A pencil! That was all I got in exchange for almost a thousand tickets. And the pencil didn't even have an eraser. He said that would be five hundred more tickets. I walked away mumbling, "Curse you, pizza dude!" What I didn't know until I finally got to the prize counter was all these tickets I'd been saving up for years were utterly worthless.

People who are becoming love stop collecting tickets. They don't do nice things for Jesus thinking they'll get a bunch of tickets they can trade someday for an eraser full of grace. This is because they don't think grace is something we can trade good conduct for. They don't take the bait and collect what has no value to God. They shun all the attention because they don't need it anymore. They realize bright lights don't need spotlights. Instead, they see every act of selfless love as a declaration of their faith. They've come to see love as its own reward simply because it pleases God.

These same people who are becoming love stop keeping track of other people's tickets too. Instead of evaluating what others are doing, they see them as people who are on their own adventure with God. They don't stop counting because they don't care; they're just so busy engaging in what God is doing in the world, it doesn't matter anymore.

There's an organization I started years ago. The website said something about how we were saving a whole generation of Ugandans. At one point, I had to ask myself why I felt like I needed to overstate what we were doing. A whole generation? Really? I don't think so. We had five hundred kids in school out of a country of forty-four million. People like me who overstate the good we've done usually do so because we're looking for validation. We're ticket counters. I was making a big deal out of my small acts of kindness. I didn't have a bad or malicious intent, just a confused one. People who are ticket counters are insecure about how much God loves us, so we mistakenly try to quantify how much we love Him back by offering Him success or accomplishments or status or titles. Here's the problem: these are just a bunch of tickets that mean nothing to Him. He wants our hearts, not our help.

That same awkward website also said we were "serving the poorest of the poor." It sounded like I was stepping over poor people and calling them posers while searching for the "poorest of the poor" so we could help them instead. My insecurity had me sounding like it was nobler to help the poorest of the poor, rather than just the merely poor. I'm sure heaven grimaces every time I do things like this. What I had done was make it about me, yet again, and our lives will never be about Jesus if we keep making everything about ourselves.

If we're going to change, we need to take some of the familiar words describing what we're doing and trade those words in for the ones Jesus used. For instance, I'm usually serving people right up until I tell everyone about how I'm serving everybody. When I do, I make it about me. We don't need to go on "mission trips" any longer. Jesus' friends never called them this. They knew love already had a name.

I've known some remarkable and courageous missionaries. Perhaps you have too. But for many, when they think of missionaries, they think of Spaniards with chest armor, a galleon, and the flu—and then all the indigenous people die. Instead of saying you're a missionary, why not just go somewhere to learn about your faith from the people you find there and be as helpful as you can be? The neat part is most of the people I know who go on "mission trips" are already doing exactly that. We don't need to call everything we do "ministry" anymore either. Just call it Tuesday. That's what people who are becoming love do.

Saving a whole generation? The poorest of the poor? Serving? Missionaries? Ministry? Before I started getting pickier about what I was saying, I made everything all about me. Yet Jesus' message to the world is as simple as it is challenging: It's not about us anymore; it's about Him. There's nothing wrong with matching shirts and wristbands. We just don't need them anymore. People who are turning into love don't need all the spin, because they aren't looking for applause or validation from others any longer. They've experienced giving away God's love as its own reward. They also don't need to write "Jesus" as the return address of every loving thing they've done. People who are turning into love give their love away freely without any thought about who gets credit for it. Jesus doesn't need credit, and we shouldn't either. When the heavens themselves declare His glory, He doesn't need our endorsement.

Some people will tell you how many times they've talked about Jesus to someone else during the day as if they're keeping count. I'm not really sure why. If I kept track of the times I mentioned Sweet Maria the way some people do about Jesus, she would think I was nuts. I can't imagine coming home and saying, "Honey, I mentioned your name five times today. Once by the water cooler and another time to someone who was going through a really hard time, and three other times on a corner to people I didn't know."

She'd probably pause graciously for a minute, check my pupils to see if I was on drugs, and then sadly ask me, "You're counting?" Keeping track of how many times I'd mentioned Sweet Maria wouldn't be evidence of a terrific marriage. It would be evidence of a whacked relationship.

What if we simply talked about the things we love? People do that with sports and cars and music and food. None of them keep track of how many times they talk about these things. We talk about what we love the most. People who are becoming love talk a lot more about what God's doing than what they're doing because they've stopped keeping score.

The next time you're tempted to boast, just say under your breath, "It's not about me." Say it a dozen times a day. Say it a thousand times a month. Say it when you wake up and when you go to sleep. Say it again and again: "It's not about me. It's not about me." Say it when you bless a meal or do something wonderful or selfless or when you help hurting people. Make it your anthem and your prayer. When we keep track of the good we've done or love people with an agenda, it's no longer love; it's just a bunch of tickets. We can either keep track of all the good we've done or all the good God's done. Only one will really matter to us. In the end, none of us wants to find out we traded the big life Jesus talked about for a box full of worthless acknowledgment.

One of the challenges I have in not keeping track of everything I've done for Jesus is that I remember everything. I don't try to; I just do. I feel like Rain Man. I remember every kind thing I've ever done for anyone. There's a bigger problem. I remember everyone who's ever wronged me or done something I thought was unfair. I'm a lawyer. I guess it just comes with the turf. I've taken and passed the bar exam in three states on the first try. For one of them, I only studied for a week and a half before taking it. The reason? I can memorize things. And that's gotten in the way of me becoming love, because people who turn into love don't keep track anymore. They don't memorize the good or bad they or anyone else have done. They memorize grace instead. Jesus didn't do any of the relational math either. He just became Love, and the world's never been the same.

The promise of love and grace in our lives is this: Our worst day isn't bad enough, and our best day isn't good enough. We're invited because we're loved, not because we earned it.

CHAPTER 9

From the Lighthouse Window

*Everyone hits a couple of wrong
notes; keep playing your song.*

My parents made me take piano lessons when I was young. It wasn't a discussion. They said it would be good for me—kind of like spinach for my fingers. Once a week, an ancient woman in a pastel cardigan would sit next to me at the piano with perfect posture, looking over my shoulder as I fumbled over the keys. She always seemed to be wearing a frown, as if it was tattooed on her face. Every sour note was made worse by her scowls, grimaces, and disapproving grunts. Sometimes I would miss notes on purpose, just to see her wrinkled face fold up like origami.

After six months of practicing, it was time for my first recital. There would be two of us playing that night: Greg and me. Greg went to my elementary school and had the same stuffy piano teacher I had. We were going to play the same tune. Even though I had been practicing for much longer, I knew he'd end up playing the song better. Greg was the kind of kid who was good at everything. He was the most talented and confident guy at the elementary school and somehow commanded a room when he entered it. He played sports, did math, gave speeches, traded corn futures, rebuilt engines—and he was only nine.

Greg arrived at the recital in a tux with monogrammed sleeves and a creased handkerchief in his pocket. He sat up straight at the piano, flipped his tails behind him, and elegantly played a song called "From the Lighthouse Window." He played so flawlessly I thought he must be the magical offspring of Beethoven and Elton John. His fingers were perfectly curled like an American bald eagle. He even crossed his hands over each other as he played, like they do in the movies. As he hit the last chord, he lifted both clawed hands over his head. He stayed in that pose for an oddly long time as the room exploded in applause. Greatness had just arrived on earth—it was Greg.

It was my turn next. I walked onstage in checkered pants and an itchy sweater my mom bought for me. I looked like Mr. Rogers. I glanced up at the audience members, who were leaning forward with great anticipation after Greg's epic performance. Then I looked down at the keys. There were so many of them. I didn't remember whether I was supposed to start on the black ones or the white ones, so I started on both and fumbled my way through the song. It was truly awful. There was no lighthouse. There was no window.

My rendition was full of mistakes, awkward pauses, and do-overs. It took me twice as long to finish the song as it had taken Greg. Instead of finishing with clawed fingers over my head, I plunked my forehead on the keys, my arms hanging limp, and I sobbed. I was so ashamed. Charlie Brown couldn't have looked more pitiful. A few people clapped to break the awkward silence as I walked offstage with my head hung low. I was humiliated. That was the day I quit playing piano.

Years later, in college, I lived in a dorm across from the music building. There was a big auditorium and a black grand piano on the stage. I passed by the auditorium several times each day on my way to and from classes. Sometimes I'd peek inside to see if anyone was playing the grand piano, but nobody ever was. Seeing the piano brought back painful memories of my embarrassing recital from so many years before. To me, it looked like a hearse with white and black keys. It reminded me of the day when I failed in front of everyone.

One day, for no particular reason, I pushed open the door to the auditorium, walked down the aisle between hundreds of empty red velvet seats, got on the stage, and sat at the piano. I didn't have on checkered pants or a cardigan sweater, but I immediately felt like I was that same kid, scared to start playing again and terrified I'd stop if I did. Nevertheless, I decided I'd make another run at "From the Lighthouse Window."

I sat up straight, curled my fingers like Greg had, and started playing. And you know what? I nailed it. I hit every note perfectly. If it had been the Olympics, there would have been confetti everywhere and people would have been lighting torches, doing flips off bars, and spiking themselves into the mats while judges held up double-digit numbers. I bet a picture of me sitting at a huge piano probably would have ended up on a box of cereal.

It had been more than ten years since my fateful piano recital. I had no sheet music. I hadn't even thought about "From the Lighthouse Window" or played a piano in as long. Yet still, I played it flawlessly. Finishing the last few stanzas, I pounded out the last chord, bringing both of my hands crashing down on the keys like I was a Viking. My fingers landed with undeniable power and authority and passion. Slowly, I lifted my clawed fingers over my head and then held them there for a really long time.

I wondered, *How could this be?*

Simple.

No audience, no spotlights.

And a lot of finger memory.

The difference between great improvisational jazz and great classical recitals is simple: in the first, there are no wrong notes. If someone makes a mistake, nobody cares or even notices. Everyone just keeps tapping their feet. In recitals, however, everyone expects perfection.

We spend a lot more time doing recitals in our faith communities than I think Jesus had in mind. Stages, audiences, and platforms change us. People who are becoming love don't need any of it. It's not inherently bad to have all the stages, but we can end up playing to the wrong audience.

My friends and I have been trying a live-event experiment called "Living Room." It's a place that doesn't have any stages. We had the first one at our home in San Diego, and we didn't give any details.

We didn't tell anyone who was going to be there, who would speak, who would play music, or what we were going to do if they came. We just said everyone was invited. This is the way Jesus did it. After Jesus went to heaven, His friends invited everyone to their living rooms too. They broke bread together and had things in common. That's what we were aiming for. Even though I'm very outgoing in public, Sweet Maria and I are pretty private people, so the idea of inviting strangers into our house was a little unsettling. Particularly for Sweet Maria, who is more introverted. We had no idea if someone would come out of our bedroom wearing my boxers and carrying her umbrella.

We set the day and time to sign up and said we could fit about thirty people in our living room, but we could squeeze sixty in. When the time came, more than eight hundred people signed up in four minutes. The ones we could fit came over, and we had a terrific time together. For the rest, we rented the House of Blues next to Disneyland a short time later. I called a few more friends to come and speak and play music. Then we handed out tickets to Disneyland, where we did our breakout sessions. The people who wanted to talk about their futures met one of the speakers in Tomorrowland. The ones who wanted to talk about their biggest fears met at the Haunted Mansion. A friend of mine who works with the homeless was on Main Street. Another who is a rapper was at Sleeping Beauty's Castle. I, of course, was by Tom Sawyer Island. I was reminded that where we meet matters as much as what we say, maybe even more. Some of the best conversations we could be having are happening at the wrong places.

We had another event to bring people together. We didn't pick the most popular city in the country; we picked one of the least popular ones. It reminded us about how God didn't pick Jerusalem. He picked relatively unappreciated places like Bethlehem and Nazareth to gather people around Jesus. I put up our house as collateral, and we rented the convention center. An amazing group of musicians and speakers agreed to come for little more than pizza and directions home. Thousands of people came, and we put lots of their money in a huge bowl. We told people if they needed some to take it and if they had more than they needed to put some in. We left the money out overnight for the convention center staff in case they needed it. When we were done, we gave away all the money from the event to people who were poor and hurting and needed some help. This is what the early church did. They made their own economy by making themselves and their resources available to everyone. They did this because they were becoming love.

Whether we want to or not, we end up memorizing what we do repeatedly. It's the way we were wired from the factory. Because this is how we're made, it's a great idea to pick actions worth repeating. People who are turning into love do this. They adopt beautiful patterns and surrounding imagery for their lives. They fill their lives with songs, practices, and habits that communicate love, acceptance, grace, generosity, whimsy, and forgiveness. People who are becoming love repeat these actions so often they don't even realize they're doing it anymore. It's just finger memory to them.

They don't need anyone to clap for them. They don't need validation for things they know are inherently right and true and beautiful. They don't need all the accolades that come with recognition. They also don't feel a need to criticize people who have gotten a couple of things wrong or hit a couple of sour chords in their lives.

I don't know about you, but I've gotten to the end of the day more than a few times and realized my untucked shirt was uneven at the bottom. I'm usually just one button off but sometimes two. The fact is, some of the people who have shaped my faith the most were a couple of buttons off on theirs. They've made some big mistakes. Run toward these people, not away. There is a quiet confidence in knowing we all hit a couple of wrong notes here and there. The report card on our faith is how we treat one another when we do.

Mary ran to the tomb a couple of days after Jesus had been buried and rose again, and she thought Jesus was the gardener. He didn't embarrass her in front of everybody and tell her all the reasons why she was wrong. He didn't have a Bible study with her about it either. Do you know what He did? He just said her name. "Mary." That's all. It was the shortest sermon ever given. We don't need to send the archers to the tower to protect baby Jesus every time someone hits a wrong note. Read the book of Revelation. He's out of the crib. Should we have a firm grip on doctrine and know what the Bible speaks to the world? You bet. Keep this in mind, though: loving people the way Jesus did is always great theology.

Memorize that. Memorize grace. Make it your finger memory. Lose the stages. Your faith isn't a recital. Speak some jazz into people's lives when they miss a couple of notes. Run to them. Don't give them advice; say their names. And if you don't know their names, don't say a thing. Because God makes people, and people make issues, but people aren't issues. They're not projects either. People are people.

The next time someone near you messes up, pull them aside in private. Don't give them a pile of instructions like it's sheet music. Just give them a hug. You'll be making grace and love and acceptance finger memory for them too.

CHAPTER 10

Three Green Lights

We don't need as much confirmation
as we think we do.

I spend a lot of time on planes. I mean, a lot. People are everywhere, and I like to be with people, so planes are just a part of my life. Last year I flew almost a half million miles. They call me "Mr. G" at the local airport. I've helped ticket agents with adoptions. I've celebrated high school graduations and mourned tremendous losses with the people who work at the airport. Sometimes I feel like Tom Hanks in the movie *The Terminal*. I had always wondered who in the world would shop for clothes in one of the airport stores. I'm a little embarrassed to admit to you—I'm that guy.

I'm a pilot, which means sometimes I fly myself to places too. I usually do this when the place I'm going is close by air and I don't want to take a long drive. Once, I had just come off an intense stretch of cross-country trips. I think I flew over Kansas at least six times in one week. I'm pretty sure I saw a farmer wave to me as I passed overhead. When I realized the next place I needed to be was a long way by car but there was a shortcut over some mountains by flying, I decided to save myself from California traffic and take a small airplane instead. I called a friend who was a member of a flying club, and he got me a deal—I could rent a plane for a hundred dollars an hour. That was just a few bucks more than Hertz. Granted, it was kind of a junky plane, but hey, it flew. So I took it.

I got a chart before I left for the airfield and threw together a quick flight plan. When I first started flying, I wasn't sure what a flight plan was. I figured mine was pretty simple—to get there and get back without hitting anything. It turns out whenever you're going to take to the skies, the first thing you do is figure out the tallest obstacle in your flight path. This is mainly so you don't die. On the way to Palm Springs the tallest thing was a six-thousand-foot mountain, so I flew over at eight thousand feet to be safe.

Just after I landed and taxied to the hangar, two guys flying an F-16 landed their fighter jet and taxied to a stop next to me. They got out wearing olive green Top Gun suits covered with oxygen hoses, flare guns, and cool patches. The sunlight hitting the pilots created a halo effect, making them look that much cooler. Meanwhile, I got out of my airplane wearing torn jeans, an old T-shirt, and a Mickey Mouse watch. I try not to compare myself with other people, but it couldn't be avoided. I glanced back at my pitiful airplane with duct tape hanging from the wings, parked next to their F-16 with missiles hanging from theirs. I felt so inadequate.

I struck up a conversation with the fighter pilots, kind of hoping I'd get to shoot one of their flare guns. I learned they had flown two thousand miles to Palm Springs so they could practice flying through the nearby valleys. They said flying through the valleys made them better pilots. It tests their skill and their teamwork. It sharpens their reaction time. I thought back to how I had made my flight plan. I had flown two thousand feet over the highest mountaintops because I wanted to be safe; these pilots flew through the valleys because they wanted to get better.

What I've come to learn so far about my faith is Jesus never asked anyone to play it safe. We were born to be brave. There's a difference between playing it safe and being safe. A lot of people think playing it safe and waiting for all the answers before they move forward is the opposite of dangerous. I disagree. If our life and our identity are found in Jesus, I think we can redefine safe as staying close to Him. Don't get me wrong. Playing it safe and waiting for assurances in our lives isn't necessarily bad; it just isn't faith anymore.

Playing it safe doesn't move us forward or help us grow; it just finds us where we are and leaves us in the same condition it found us in. God wants something different for us. His goal is never that we'll come back the same. He's hoping we'll return more dependent on Him. I'm not saying everything needs to be risky in our lives, but we'd be well served if a few more things were riskier in our faith. Loving people we don't understand or agree with is just the kind of beautiful, counterintuitive, risky stuff people who are becoming love do.

Every day we get to decide if we'll take it easy and fly over the mountaintops in our relationships or make ourselves better and find our way through the valleys. Heaven and a world full of hurting people are hoping we will. The Bible talks about this. It says when our faith gets tested, we have the chance to grow. This makes sense to me. Stated differently, if we want our faith to get stronger, we need to navigate some deep places.

It sounds simple on paper, but in real life it's a lot tougher than it looks. I'm a pretty upbeat guy, and while I'm willing to go through a valley or two, I don't aim for them the way those fighter pilots did. The truth is, I only reluctantly go through difficult times or deal with difficult people. When I do, I'm quick to complain to myself about what a raw deal I got and how unfair it is for such a nice guy like me to have such hard things happen or have to deal with such difficult people. People who are becoming love understand God guides us into uncomfortable places because He knows most of us are too afraid to seek them out ourselves. It happens to me all the time, and I usually only recognize in hindsight that the hard places I've navigated helped me steer a more purposeful course forward. This has been God's idea for us all along.

When I finished the event in Palm Springs, it was late in the evening, around ten o'clock. I drove back to the local airport and readied my plane for takeoff. The F-16 was gone, and I imagined those guys were going Mach 5 through a nearby valley, getting better, testing their skills, and having the time of their lives. But me? I was just ready for bed.

The flight home was uneventful. I didn't do any barrel rolls or weave through any canyons. When I got near the airport in my hometown, I went through the landing procedures and checklists.

One of the last steps was pulling the lever to lower the landing gear. There are green lights on the control panel to let the pilot know each wheel is completely down, locked, and ready to hit the runway. When you see three green lights on the panel, you're ready to land.

I pulled the lever and could hear the wheels rotating into position, then something happened I wasn't counting on. I only got two green lights—one for each of the back two wheels. There was no green light for the nose gear. I wasn't tired anymore. I called the control tower, trying to play it cool.

"Tower, I don't think I have a nose wheel."

"This is the tower. Copy. Please fly by the tower. I'll try to get a visual on your landing gear."

I adjusted my flight path to "buzz the tower." I felt like Tom Cruise in *Top Gun*, except it was dark and no one could see me. When I had flown past the tower, the controller called back over the radio.

"This is the tower. It's too dark. I can't tell if the gear's down."

Wait, what? That's it? That's all he had to say? I wanted to yell back over the radio, "What do you mean you can't tell? You're the guy in the control tower. You're supposed to know stuff!"

After a minute or two, the controller came on the radio again and told me to fly by the tower again, so I did. Once again, he told me he couldn't tell. I was stuck with just my two green lights.

Another few long minutes passed, and he crackled through the radio again. "Are you declaring an emergency?"

Chuckling, I said, "Buddy, I declared an emergency in my shorts about fifteen minutes ago."

My mind was working furiously to figure out how I could get out of this. None of the options I could think of sounded very attractive. If I landed the plane without a nose gear, it wouldn't end well. If I stayed in the air, I'd run out of fuel and it'd probably end worse. If I didn't get to a bathroom soon, well, we all know how that would end.

We've all had circumstances like this in our lives. We bank on one thing happening and it doesn't. A job. A date. A bonus. An answer. A verdict. We're all waiting for more information, more confirmation, more certainty at some point. Sometimes anything more will do. We want clarity and instead we get confusion. We want answers and we just get more questions. We make terrific plans and then something unexpected comes up and they end up in a pile on the floor like dirty laundry. Perhaps we were hoping a door would open or another would close. We're hoping something we desperately need to end would be over, or something else we want to start would begin. All the signs pointed in one direction, then in an instant, something went wrong. The flight plan we laid out for ourselves took us high over the mountaintops, but the one we actually got flung us deep into the valleys.

In short, most of us want more green lights than we have. It's easy to forget that our faith, life, and experiences are all the green lights we need. What we need to do is to stop circling the field and get the plane on the ground. God doesn't allow these kinds of things to happen to mess with our heads; He uses these circumstances to shape our hearts. He knows difficulties and hardship and ambiguity are what cause us to grow because we are reminded of our absolute dependence upon Him.

God's plans aren't ruined just because our plans need to

change. What if we found out God's big plan for our lives is that we wouldn't spend so much of our time trying to figure out a big plan for our lives? Perhaps He just wants us to love Him and love each other. Our ability to change is often blocked by our plans. Some people look for shooting stars or ladybugs landing on their noses as answers from God. Sure, He could communicate to us this way. But honestly, while these kinds of things have happened to me, they've never really felt like answers; they just felt like reminders.

I don't think God uses card tricks to get our attention. Rather, He gives us hopes and dreams and desires. He gives us tenacity and resilience and courage. He's made us good at some things and horrible at other things. He brings joyful, beautiful, fun people into our lives and a few difficult ones too. Sometimes He changes the trajectory of our plans by taking away what we've comfortably known and letting us fly through valleys that are deeper and narrower than any we've been through before.

Don't ignore the green lights you already have. What delights you? What fires your imagination? What fills you with a deep sense of meaning and purpose? What draws you closer to God? What is going to last in your life and in the lives of others? Do those things. They're your green lights. Most of us already have more lights than we need. Don't wait to join a movement. A movement is just a bunch of people making moves. Be a movement. Figure out what your next move is going to be, then make it. No one is remembered for what they only planned to do.

I only got two green lights in the airplane when I wanted three. You may want ten green lights before you do the risky thing God has for you to do, but you only have eight. I once heard a friend say all opportunities come with expiration dates. If you don't grasp the opportunity in front of you, it's likely going to go away at some point. Here's the deal: All those deep urgings you feel to step toward the beautiful, courageous thing you're afraid to do—you probably won't always have the chance. Now is the time. Your life, your experiences, and your faith are your green lights. Make your move.

The procedure for landing a plane without nose gear is different than normal, as you might expect. You land on the back wheels first, so you know they are down and locked. Life's rules aren't much different. Figure out the couple of things you're sure about and put all your weight on those things. I've put all of mine on Jesus because I figured out He was a green light I could trust. But it doesn't end there. God has surrounded me with countless people, just like He has you. Plenty of those people are trustworthy lights who point me to Jesus through our relationships. Find those people in your life and lean on them a little. Be more vulnerable and transparent than you think you have the wheels for. Do it anyway. Sometimes when we ask God for an answer, He sends us a friend. Figure out who He's already sent to you.

There are plenty of questions I still have. I usually don't have all the green lights I'd like. There's probably a lot you don't have nailed down yet either. Be honest with yourself about these things. God is less concerned about the people who admit their doubts than the ones who pretend they're certain. Each day I start with the things I'm certain about and try to land my weight on those things. It always starts with a loving, caring God who is tremendously interested in me and the world I live in. I'm picky about what else I add after that.

I didn't know if the wheels on the plane would work, but I knew God was with me as I fretted about my landing gear. The tower had pretty much gone silent on me. It made sense. We'd said just about all we had to say, and words can't turn into wheels. It's in those times where it feels like everything has been said that I seem to sense God's presence more clearly. I don't know what the guy in the tower was doing while I was sweating bullets and waiting either to explode or screech down the runway, a flurry of sparks and screams. I know what God was doing, though. He was with me.

I finished my approach and passed the first white lines on the landing strip. It was time for me to prepare for touchdown. I brought the plane down as slowly as I could with the nose of the plane as high as possible. I closed my eyes briefly and exhaled. It was time to see what would happen.

The plane floated closer to the ground and the rear wheels touched down. As the nose of the plane came down, I found myself counting down: *three . . . two . . . one . . .*

When I reached zero, there would either be a lot of propellers hitting a lot of concrete or a small bounce indicating the front wheel was down and locked. Either way, I was a bystander at this point.

I reached zero in my mental countdown.

There was a bounce. The front wheel was there.

I started whooping and hollering and laughing.

Get this: it turned out what had me all twisted while I was in the air was a burned-out five-cent light bulb.

I spent far too much time circling the field that night because I didn't get all the green lights I wanted. I think a lot of us do the same thing with much of our lives too. Don't let a nickel light bulb keep you from fulfilling your purpose. God isn't surprised we want more confirmation. He just hopes we won't get stuck waiting for it.

Who wouldn't want more green lights? Yet, at some point, we need to stop waiting for permission and go live our lives. God isn't stingy with His love, and He doesn't delight in seeing us uncomfortable either. Perhaps we don't get all the answers and confirmations we ask for because God loves seeing us grow.

In the same breath, though, sometimes it's a good thing to pause. One of the writers in the Bible said to his friends that just because the door was open didn't mean it was for him to walk through. The difference between a prudent pause and persistent paralysis is a distinction worth knowing.

Recognize when your beautiful ambitions are getting stuck inside your head. You don't need to take all the steps, just the next one. God may not give us all the green lights we want, but I'm confident He gives us all the green lights He wants us to have at the time. Go with what you've got. If God wants you to stay put, He'll let you know. We also have some guaranteed green lights that are always on: our noble desires; God's clear instructions in the Bible to love everybody, always; His love for us; and the gift of each other. You can put a lot of weight on these and triangulate from there to figure out the rest of life's unknowns.

The difference between the number of green lights we want and the number we get from God is a pretty good description of what faith is. Faith isn't knowing what we can't see; it's landing the plane anyway, rather than just circling the field. Get the plane on the ground.

CHAPTER 11

Last One, Best One

Jesus often uses our blind spots
to reveal Himself to us.

I regularly visit Northern Iraq to check on one of the schools
where our organization, Love Does, helps young children find
safety and a loving environment in a war zone. If you keep up with
the news, you know the Middle East is a really rough place with
lots of turmoil. Northern Iraq is no different, and we do all we
can to help these kids get a different vision for the future of their
lives. A couple of terrific organizations and a few families decided
to move there and be with these kids and the people in the communities where they serve. I love seeing the kids thrive when just
weeks or months earlier they didn't know where they'd get their
next meal or where they'd sleep that night.

With our friends, we run schools for hundreds of kids dis-
placed by the civil wars. We have a hospital, a school with hundreds
of Yazidi and refugee kids, and homes we've built for refugees from

Syria. We've met with Peshmerga fighters on the front lines as they battled ISIS soldiers we could see from behind sandbags a short distance away. The name Peshmerga means "the people who confront death." It's an apt description of these brave men.

We've given these brave Peshmerga fighters medals to let them know how proud we are of them. One time while at the front lines, one of the generals invited us to come into his tent where they had laid out a battle plan for retaking Mosul, a city of two million people. I couldn't wait to see the detailed maps and plans and satellite images I imagined were inside. Surprisingly, there were none of those. Instead, there was an eight-by-twelve-foot sandbox with some plastic army men, tanks, roads, and small white and black flags on it. I thought there would be more to it.

Here's the thing: we usually don't need all the plans we make. Sure, plans can help from time to time, but planning to love people is different than just loving people. For some people, it's easier to make plans than to make time. If this is you, here's how to fix it: make love your plan. There's less to write down that way.

During one of my trips to Northern Iraq, I woke up one morning and couldn't see out of my right eye. It was weird. I kept moving my hand back and forth covering my left eye first, then my right eye. I rubbed my eyes and shook my head a few times, but it didn't help. There wasn't anything there. I could have stared at the sun and not seen a thing. I had five more countries in the Middle East and Asia to be in before returning home, so like a dummy I just kept going, thinking I'd get it sorted out later. No brains, no head-ache. It was a bad move.

When I got home, I went to see the eye doctor. She's one of the world's best and told me I was the stupidest smart guy she'd ever met. I'm sure she was overstating it, and I was probably only tied for last. I had already decided if I'd done so much damage that I needed a fake eye, I'd want to get an assortment to pick from. I wanted one with a laser in it, like the guy in *The Terminator*, and also one that was a hairy eyeball I could slip into place for anyone who really irritated me.

They've done quite a few operations on my eye since I had my problem. Before every operation, I always ask my eye doctor how much I'll be able to see afterward. You know what? She's never told me. Instead, each time she just says, "Bob, you're going to see more." At first I felt like she was dodging the question. I was looking for a prognosis for my eye, but she gave me something far better. I got a promise from someone I could trust and a reminder about my life. It's the same promise God gives us every day. We want God to tell us all the details, but all we usually get is a prom-ise that we'll see more of Him if we look in the right places. This doctor knows what she's doing. She practically invented eyes. Jesus knows what He's doing, too, and He *did* invent eyes. Because I trust both of them, I'm okay with the promise I'll see more.

We'll see what we spend the most time looking for.

My eyesight is slowly coming back. It will no doubt take some time to be fully restored. I'm not sure how much sight I'll get back and how long it will last. I've only had a half-dozen operations so far. I'm going for a world record. While I wait, I've already seen what Jesus and the doctor said would come true, even if my eyesight isn't fully restored yet. I'm seeing more.

There have been more than a couple of benefits of missing sight in one eye. For instance, I know where my blind spot is. It's half. Right-hand turns at intersections these days are spotty at best. It's like playing rock-paper-scissors. I usually just roll down my windows and yell, "Coming through!" Then I hit the gas.

When I read the stories in the Bible about the blind people Jesus met, I can identify with them a little more. The one I probably relate to the most is the guy who got his sight healed twice. After Jesus touched this guy the first time, He asked him what he could see. The man told Jesus, "I see people; they look like trees walking around." Jesus touched his eyes a second time, and it was only after the second touch that he could see things the way they really were. First touches, like first impressions, are great, but I think a lot of us need a second touch.

There are quite a few people who may have bumped into Jesus along the way, but it didn't stick the first time. It's not a failed attempt when it happens, just like Jesus didn't mess up the miracle the first time He touched the guy's eyes. God wants us to be real with Him about the effect He's had in our lives. I'll level with you: if I were the blind guy in the story, I would have been tempted to lie to Jesus after the first touch and tell Him I was healed. You know, just so Jesus wouldn't look bad. But what Jesus is looking for are honest answers about what's really going on in our lives, not a bunch of spin. The reason is simple. If the guy without sight had faked it and said he could see everything just fine after the first touch, he wouldn't have been actually healed.

The truth is, we don't really know why Jesus touched this man's eyes twice. I think some of the miracles God does in our lives happen in stages. Even though we've been touched by God, we still don't see people for who they are until something more happens in us. It's not trees we confuse them for; it's opinions and positions, social issues and status, titles and accomplishments and behaviors.

Having a problem with my eye has helped me understand Jesus a little better in other ways. I've been asking Him to help me see and know more about the things I don't understand in my life and the lives of other people. Most of the time, I receive an indirect answer or no answer at all. Some people explained to me early on about how not getting an answer from God really is an answer. I suppose they could be right, but honestly, I never really bought it. If I sent someone a letter and didn't get an answer, I'd wonder if they really got it. Sometimes when we ask for an answer, God sends us a companion. They often come in blue jeans, but they could also be wearing a stethoscope and a white doctor's coat.

Because I trust Jesus even more than I trust the eye doctor, I'm becoming more comfortable with the promise from God that I'm going to see more. Even if it takes a couple more touches. A small but important change these days is that I assume everyone can see more than I can, and I'm usually right. Maybe I won't see as much as I'd like to see right now, but I'm okay with knowing I'll see more. It gives me something to look forward to.

Keep your eyes fixed on Jesus—or your one eye, if you don't have two that work. He sees who we're becoming, and He wants us to become love.

I have a friend named Lex. He has the same problem in both of his eyes that I have in one of mine. After ten failed operations, he lost his eyesight completely when he was eight years old. In high school Lex began to compete in track-and-field events. By the time he got to college, he figured out he could run like the wind. So he went out for the track team. My first thought was, *How can a blind guy run track?* Then I found out Lex has a friend. His friend runs in front of Lex and calls his name. Lex just runs toward a voice he knows he can trust.

Everyone who runs track-and-field picks an event. Lex picked the long jump. This still makes my head spin. If you're not familiar with this event, you run as fast as you can down a three-foot-wide track from a position more than one hundred feet away. With your last step, you launch into the air as high as you can from a wooden board in the track and land as far away as you can in a sand pit. Impossible for a blind guy, right? Not for Lex. Do you know why? He's got a friend whose voice he knows he can trust.

What Lex does is both simple and impossible at the same time. When it's his turn to compete, his friend squares Lex's shoulders to the sand pit down the track, then goes to the edge of the pit and starts yelling, "Fly! Fly! Fly!" over and over. Lex runs toward his friend's voice as fast as he can and then jumps as far as he's able.

Get this: Lex went out for the US Paralympic team—and he made it. He can jump farther than just about anyone in the world. Here's the reason why: people who are becoming love try impossible things because they've surrounded themselves with voices they can trust.

At the World Championships, Lex's friend took him to the far end of the narrow track. He squared Lex's shoulders and walked back to the edge of the sand pit. Then he started calling, "Fly! Fly! Fly!" to Lex. Because Lex is blind, he doesn't always run in a straight line. The louder his friend called out to Lex, the more Lex wandered. When Lex got to the end of the track, he leaped into the air with everything he had. The problem? His path had wandered, and he launched crooked. Everyone in the stadium gasped. Lex missed the sandpit entirely and crashed and burned on the concrete. Lex's friend put his hands over his head in disbelief at what had just happened as he ran to his friend's side. Lex was badly bruised, his track uniform was ripped, and he was helped off the field for medical attention.

We're all a little blind and have a tendency to wander. Sometimes we know what caused us to stop running in a straight line, and other times we don't. We crash and burn and usually don't know what happened. It's what happens next that will tell a lot about who we're becoming.

I'm no athlete, but if I were Lex, I would have been tempted to quit. I would have thought about how unfair my life was. I'd complain to myself about how I'd jumped far and hit hard. I might be afraid if it happened once, it might happen again. These are the voices of defeat each of us hears at some point. If we let them, these dissonant voices can drown out the voices we've come to trust in our lives. Lex doesn't see the world this way. His faith doesn't just inform his heart; it informs his whole life.

Lex's friend got him a new uniform so he didn't moon everyone, and Lex walked back onto the field to thunderous applause. Together, they walked to the end of the narrow runway. There's a saying in track: "Last one, best one." His friend squared Lex's shoulders and his feet once again, walked to the edge of the sand pit, and called, "Fly! Fly! Fly!" as he clapped faster and faster. When Lex hit the board on his sixteenth step, he leaped into the air like a gazelle. When he hit the sand more than twenty-one feet later, he won the whole competition. Sure, he'd strayed a little from the path before. He'd even crashed the last time he'd tried, but Lex doesn't let fear call the shots in his life, and we shouldn't either.

We've all jumped for something we couldn't see. A relationship, a career, even our faith. We've all been beat up too. We've jumped big and missed even bigger. We aim for the soft sand but hit the hard stuff. Here's the thing: God doesn't like us more when we succeed or less when we fail. He delights in our attempts. He gave each of us different abilities too. I can't jump over a street curb. Lex can leap over a Buick.

I'm not trying to be Lex, and he isn't interested in being me. One thing we do have in common is having a couple of good friends. These friends of ours don't need to give us a lot of instruction either. They just call our names. The promise Jesus made to His friends was simply this: He promised to be a voice they could trust. All He asked His friends to do was to run toward it.

Jesus talked about sheep and shepherds a lot. I've had a couple of dogs. I've even briefly had a parakeet and a turtle. But I could never really relate when Jesus talked about what it's like to have a lot of sheep. He said sheep can recognize the shepherd's voice because it's a voice they've come to trust. I think I understand a little more now what He was saying.

God doesn't just give us Himself. Sometimes He gives us a few other people in our lives whose voices we can trust. Figure out what Jesus' voice sounds like in your life. He's standing at the end of the track calling your name. Run as fast as you can in His direction.

I had Lex come and speak to a university class I teach. Hundreds of students sat spellbound as Lex spoke to them for an hour. There was a grand piano on the stage, and he even laid down a song I'm still humming. It turns out the guy has some pretty strong vocal pipes too. When class was over, we got in my car and made the forty-five-minute drive back to the Olympic training center. When I turned on my blinker to make a right turn, Lex leaned over and said, "Bob, it's the next street." I just about swerved off the road. "What?" I asked in amazement. Here's the crazy part: he was right.

"How did you know that?" I asked him, still stunned as I made the next right.

"I keep track of where I am. It helps me find what I need," he said confidently.

I've got a lot to learn from Lex. I have plenty of sight and use very little of it. He has none and somehow sees more than a dozen optometrists can. I wonder if the Bible has so many stories about blind people because many of them are in touch with where they are and what they need. Oftentimes I'm not. I'm learning from Lex the power of keeping track of where I am, figuring out what I need and listening for voices I can trust.

As we drove down the correct road, Lex asked, "Do you want me to blow your mind?"

"Buddy, it's already blown. There's nothing left," I said, shaking my head.

"There's a speed bump in thirty feet." A few moments later, both sets of tires bounced over the bump in the road.

We've all heard the term *blind faith*. I didn't understand what it really meant until I met Lex. He's the wise man who told me, "It's not what you look at; it's what you see." I agree.

Keep running your race. Is it going to be easy? Heck, no. You might even question a couple of times if it's worth it. Jesus is standing at the edge of eternity calling your name. He wants you to run toward Him as fast as your legs will carry you. He knows you can't always see what is before you, and He wants you to forget what lies behind you. *Fly! Fly! Fly!* His voice is one you can trust. He wants you to run big and jump far.

Last one, best one.

CHAPTER 12

Three Minutes at a Time

*Friendships can last a lifetime, but we
make them three minutes at a time.*

H ello, Patricia? Hi! What can I do for you?"
"Adrian's gone."

"Gone? Where did he go? Let's go find him."

"No, Adrian died today."

When I heard those words, I was stopped by a wave of confusion. How could this be? You see, Adrian had become a close friend of mine. He was particularly special to me because we built our years-long friendship just three minutes at a time. Let me tell you how.

Adrian worked at the airport in San Diego. He stood at the front of a long line of often anxious and frustrated people, waiting to get through security. Some were on their way to a vacation, and some were on business trips. Some were happy, and some were sad. It seemed weirdly incongruous; they were all heading somewhere, yet they were all going nowhere at the moment. The security lines were always too long, and I could feel the tension of a hundred snagged travelers all trying to squeeze through the security bottleneck.

Most mornings the line stretched like a giant snake out the doors of the airport. None of it was Adrian's fault, of course. Not the lateness, not the bottleneck, not all the security rules. But Adrian bore the brunt of a thousand angry stares, crumpled faces, and sharp comments every day. It wasn't because he deserved it; it was just because he was the guy at the front of the line. You see, Adrian worked for the TSA and wore a uniform two sizes too big for him. His job was to check IDs to see if people were who they said they were.

Sometimes people pop out in a crowd. It's not always because they're handsome or beautiful or the one up front or on a stage. What makes them stand out is they're not trying to get any attention at all. I'm married to one of these people. We've got three kids and their spouses, Ashley and Jon, who are these kinds of people too. It's hard to list what makes someone catch your eye in this way. It's probably a combination of many things, including humility, kindness, quiet resolve, and hard work.

Adrian stood five-foot-nothing on his tiptoes and weighed less than a bag of chips. He looked to be in his midsixties, but it was hard to tell. He was a strange mix of youthful enthusiasm, calm wisdom, and deep love. Adrian had a sturdy presence about him that came from many years of tireless work. He walked with the swagger of a high school wrestling letterman and the humbleness of a monk.

I travel quite a bit and had passed by Adrian at the front of the airport security line a dozen times over the course of a few weeks. Each time, I noticed something special about him. No matter who he met at the front of the line, Adrian always treated them with love and respect. The people in line could have been distracted by the events in their lives, frustrated by the wait, sad at leaving, or excited about arriving—it didn't matter to Adrian. He greeted everybody with his quiet and sincere brand of love, which made things somehow much better. This person I observed from afar each week fascinated me, and I knew I wanted to meet him.

Nearing the front of the line one day, I decided I'd thank this kind man for what he did each day and, in particular, for the way he welcomed strangers like me each morning. When I got to the front of the line, I reached out my right hand as I handed my ID to him with my left. "Hi, I'm Bob," I said. "I've passed by you a dozen times and I just wanted to thank you for the way you treat each person in line. It's really amazing. The way you treat people reminds me a lot of the way Jesus loved."

The small man looked up slowly from my driver's license and handed it back to me as if it were his. He didn't say a word, but I could see his eyes well up. He took a couple of small steps toward me, then he wrapped his arms around me and put his head on my chest. "I'm Adrian," he said into my sweater. I'll admit, it was more than a little awkward. But there we stood, just the two of us, slow dancing at the front of the TSA line while 150 business travelers who were late for their flights watched. This was the beginning of my friendship with Adrian, three minutes at a time. We said our goodbyes and I was already looking forward to my next trip to the airport and the next chance to learn a little bit more about him.

A few days later, I got my chance. During our next three minutes together, I found out about Adrian's wife of over forty years, Patricia. He spoke about her with a hushed reverence, the kind reserved for the pope. She was obviously the love of his life. We hadn't finished talking about Patricia, but the line moved, so I did too. I knew we would pick up our conversation where we left off the next time I got to the airport.

On subsequent trips, I found out about Adrian's son, a daughter, a grandchild, a brother, and a previous career he had with Aeromexico as an electrician. We began meeting at my house to talk about life and love and Jesus. Our families began spending Christmases together. It was terrific. One year, Adrian gave me a double-matted photograph of the main library in Mexico City and told me all the books in there couldn't contain what he had been learning about God in the past few months.

I learned Adrian was saving up money for a down payment on a small house. He told me how he spent the weekends swirling a sign over his head on a downtown corner, advertising apartments for rent to earn the extra bucks he'd need to swing the payment. I teased him about what might happen on a windy day as all one hundred pounds of him were blown across the street and into a field.

During one of our three-minute meetings, Adrian updated me on his dream house. He'd saved up enough money and thought he had found the perfect one. It would be modest by most standards, but the way Adrian described it, it was as grand as any castle in England—no doubt with a moat, a couple of drawbridges, and horsemen. Yes, lots of horsemen. Patricia was traveling up from

Mexico City, where she had been staying with their grown children, to see the house for the first time. He had warned her in advance the house was tiny, but he couldn't wait for her to see it. There was a twinkle in his eye when he spoke. No mansion would have a prouder owner.

As the line moved, we shouted over other people's heads to stretch our three minutes into four or five. Adrian had to jump as he shouted out the last details over the heads of two bald guys. He was bursting with pride. "I'm getting the house! I'm getting the house!" he shouted with his small arms waving over his head. I waved my arms over my head too. Someone in the line cheered for him. The person standing next in line in front of him gave him a hug. Love and unbridled anticipation are contagious in this way.

Over the course of the next several dozen trips through the airport, I learned Patricia loved the house, Adrian had purchased it, and Patricia was on her way to move in. He beamed as he talked about what he'd accomplished. I was so proud of him. I felt like I was getting a house too.

What I liked about Adrian the most was he knew who he was. I also was struck by how authentic he was with his growing faith. Humble people don't fall for the lies pride tries to entice us with to fake it. After a particularly bad day, God's first words in the garden to Adam and Eve were simple ones: "Where are you?" It's the first post-screwup conversation between God and the first family. God, of course, wasn't talking about geography when He asked the question, and He's not asking us about it now either. He hadn't lost track of the ones He had created and He hasn't lost track of you and me. Instead, I think God wanted Adam and Eve to figure out where they were with Him after they'd failed. He's never stopped asking us the very same question: "Where are you?" To figure out *where* we are we need to understand *who* we are. It's the question Adrian asked thousands of people every day: "Who are you?"

A lot of us pretend we're at a different place in our faith than we really are. We pretend to be someone we're not, hoping we'll find more love or respect or popularity or get more attention. There usually isn't a bad motive underlying this; we do it because we're insecure or we're looking for approval or we're reaching for a way to connect with the people around us. Yet when what our faith looks like becomes more important than what it is, it's evidence we've forgotten who we really are. God constantly allows things to happen in our lives that help us understand where we are with Him and who we really are in the context of our circumstances. It's like He's checking our IDs every day, not unlike what Adrian did at the airport.

The thing about Adrian is he was never confused about his identity. He didn't have a Facebook page where he projected who he wished he was. I never saw him take a selfie. These aren't bad things, of course, but they can lead us away from ourselves. Adrian was just a guy who loved God, loved his family, and loved the next person who was standing in front of him.

One of the stories God tells in the Bible is much simpler than we sometimes make it. Jesus was with a few of His friends and He asked them who people thought He was. It must have felt like a funny question for Jesus to ask His friends who had been with Him for a few years already. Peter spoke up first and said He thought Jesus was God. Jesus told him this wasn't the kind of thing Peter could have figured out just because someone told him what to think. Instead, He said it's something Peter would have only known because God told him. Jesus then told His friends something even more puzzling. He told them not to tell anyone who He was. At first this seems to go against the grain of the evangelistic model many of us have been exposed to, but I don't think He was trying to keep His identity a secret. Just the opposite. Jesus probably wants us to *show* people who He is by what we do, not just *tell* them what we think.

I've been asking God to help me figure out who I really am and who He really is. Here's the thing: Jesus is the only one who can let us know the truth about ourselves and the truth about who He is. Most of us have all the knowledge we need. People don't need information; they want examples. God wants to use people like us to show the world what we know about Jesus by having them see the way we love the people around us. Particularly the difficult ones.

I've sometimes thought I'd make a lousy evangelist because I don't think we lead people to Jesus. I think Jesus leads people to Jesus. Sure, we can tell the people we meet about Jesus. I talk about Him all the time because my life is His, but I don't try to talk people into Him. When I've tried and it worked, what I often found is I'd led people to me, not Him. If we take Jesus at His word, people won't know who Jesus is because we've told them; they'll know because Jesus let them know. If you're already friends with Jesus, don't get in everyone else's way as they figure it out with

Him. Just love them and point them in His direction. If you've only heard of Him, ask Him who He is. I bet He'll let you know.

When Jesus invaded history, it's as if He stood at the front of a long line of people—everyone who has ever lived or will live. He asked all of us if we knew who we were, and He asked us who we thought He was. Some got it right and some didn't. The same is still true today. I bet Jesus asked so many people about who they were, and who they thought He was, because there were as many people then as there are now who are confused about both. Our words say we're one person, but our lives say we're someone else. We do the same thing with Jesus. Some of us say He's God and we're following Him, but then we live like our ego is calling all the shots.

The beautiful message of Jesus is His invitation to everyone that they can trade in who they used to be for who God sees them becoming. He said we can each get a new identity in Him. The people who take Him up on this offer begin to define success and failure the way He did. They move from merely identifying with someone's pain to standing with them in it, and from having a bunch of opinions to giving away love and grace freely. People who are becoming love make doing these things look effortless.

With the new identity comes a new set of rules. It was a backward economy Jesus talked about. He said if people wanted to be at the front of the line, they needed to go to the back. If they wanted to be a good leader, they would need to be an even better follower. If they wanted to know Him better, they'd need to stop thinking so much about themselves, and if they wanted to love Him more, they needed to love each other more.

The last time I saw Adrian, we got some coffee and caught up. I told him I was going to be out of the country for a couple of months. After a great conversation, we hugged, said our good-byes, and he tapped a text message to each of my kids telling them how much he loved them. Adrian didn't tell them about who they used to be; he told each of them who they were becoming. Every time we do this for one another, we reaffirm our true identities.

When we draw a circle around the whole world like grace did and say everybody is in, God's love gives us bigger identities than we used to have. With our newer, bigger identities, we can draw even bigger arcs around people's lives. We start to see that our time here isn't meant to be spent forming opinions about the people we meet. It's an opportunity to draw the kind of circles around them that grace has drawn around us, until everybody is on the inside.

We don't decide who in line is in and who's out, and we don't need to waste any more time engaging in the kinds of arguments some people get sucked into. People who are becoming love don't swing at every pitch. We start by meeting people just three minutes at a time. Don't waste a minute of it arguing with people who are wrong. Quietly delight in the confidence that comes from having found truth in your own life. God never promised we'd have all the answers. What He offers to us is a box of crayons and the opportunity to let love draw bigger circles around the people we meet than they thought were possible.

The call from Patricia about Adrian's death came as a shock to us all. Apparently, Adrian walked out of the airport after work and had a game-ending stroke in the parking lot. There was no warning and no reason. It just happened. I haven't tried to figure out why. Sometimes when we search too hard for explanations, we risk making them up by mistake. I've got quite a few questions about why Adrian passed. Perhaps that's why God made eternity last so long—He knew it would take a while to explain what He was doing. Before you decide why things have happened in your past or are happening now, wait for God to whisper the reasons to you. It will be worth the wait.

Adrian left behind Patricia and the rest of his family and friends, but he also left behind far more. He changed my perspective on what it takes to make a friend and to be a friend. You see, I used to think it would take a lifetime to become someone's friend, but now I think we do it just three minutes at a time. It's the way Jesus made friends with most of the people He met, and it's a great way for us to engage the people around us, including the ones we've been avoiding.

I don't know what happens after we die. The Bible says to be apart from the body is to be present with God. Perhaps it happens in an instant, and maybe it's a little like the way it feels when you wake up from a nap. Either way, after Adrian died, I bet he opened his eyes and he was in heaven with Jesus.

I don't know what heaven is going to look like. I don't know if the roads are made of gold. Honestly, I'm kind of hoping they're covered in Dippin' Dots. I don't know if we're going to be assembled in rows, singing Chris Tomlin songs, but I kind of doubt it. I also don't know about getting a set of wings either, but I'm crossing my fingers we don't. (That might just be a guy thing.)

I don't know what color the gates of heaven are or who takes over when Saint Peter takes a day off. But I wouldn't be surprised if there will be a long line of people waiting to get in. It will wind out the door like a long snake. Somewhere near the entry at the front of the line, I'm betting there will be a guy who looks a lot like Adrian. He won't be checking for titles or degrees or accomplishments or how rich or poor someone was. He'll be asking everyone whether they found their identity in Jesus and if they *really* were who they said they were during their lives.

CHAPTER 13

Karl's Dive

We're not held back by what we don't
have, but by what we don't use.

Karl was like most other kids in high school. He loved sports, and he was good at them too. But he liked mischief even more, and he was even better at that. He and his friends would stare at the calendar, wishing their way through the spring to the summer and the chance to run wild together. Karl had a contagious charm and would quietly and unintentionally command the room when he bounced through the door. He was handsome, he was smart, and he had a well-earned reputation as a jokester. The next prank was always just around the corner for Karl and his buddies.

Some people can juggle. Others can tie a cherry stem in a knot with their tongue. Karl could hold his breath like a dolphin. He grew up on a lake in Illinois and would practice sinking in the water with his arms spread wide, no doubt hoping to score a rescue attempt and perhaps some mouth-to-mouth resuscitation from the cute girl who was the lifeguard on duty. It never really happened, but just the possibility made all the practice worth it.

Each year, Karl and his buddies would head to a couple of lakes in Wisconsin for their summer adventures. They would float through the lazy summer days swimming, sailing, skipping rocks, and meeting the occasional girl or two who were also on vacation. Meeting girls, of course, trumped all the Huckleberry Finn stuff.

One day, Karl was at a friend's house and saw two girls from his high school, whom he wanted to both scare and impress, sitting on a dock at the edge of the water. Karl thought it would take something big to wow them. He wanted to make an impression with some attention-getting bravado. So he puffed out his chest and set off running toward the shore. His plan was to startle the girls by leaping over them and making a big splash in the water. Girls apparently dig that kind of stuff. His buddies were egging him on as he ran.

When Karl got to the end of the dock, he leaped like he'd been shot out of a cannon. As he passed over the heads of the girls, he gave out a loud battle cry and looked down to see their faces. His head pointed him downward and his body followed. Karl hit the water like a lawn dart and made a big splash. His buddies ran up to the girls as they giggled, offering them towels. The plan had worked perfectly. The girls looked over the edge of the dock into the murky water, anticipating Karl would come bursting out.

As usual, Karl acted like a submarine just a foot under the surface of the water. He was pulling the trick he'd perfected over the years by lying still. As one minute passed, the girls' giggles faded into concern. "Shouldn't we do something?"

Soon, concern turned into panic. This wasn't funny any longer. Karl was still motionless below the surface. Even his buddies thought Karl was taking his stunt a little too far. They jumped feet first into the murky lake, and to their surprise the water barely covered their knees. The water Karl had jumped into headfirst was only three feet deep.

One of his buddies grabbed Karl by the ankles while another grabbed him by the shoulders. As they lifted Karl onto the dock, his neck flopped back like a rag doll. Fortunately, a paramedic lived across the street, and a friend who saw the commotion called for an ambulance. Karl was whisked away to the hospital.

Spinal cords are tricky things. They're made up of a bundle of nerves that control most of our bodies. Our spinal cords control our sense of touch, how our arms and legs move, how our lungs work, and much more. When the spinal cord is injured, messages no longer get from the brain to the parts of our body below the injury. With any spinal cord injury, there's damage done immediately and then more damage as the injury begins to shut down other parts of the body. It's like a dangerous game of dominoes. The spinal cord is so specialized it can't repair itself, and even the most skilled doctor can do very little to help.

At the hospital, the doctors tried to assess the extent of Karl's injuries. They asked him if he knew where he was, who the president was, and what month Christmas was celebrated in. Karl could talk for the first forty hours following his injury, but then he lost his ability to speak as his spinal cord continued to swell. He had many questions, but he had been stripped of the ability to ask them. Karl felt as if he'd been padlocked inside his body.

A nurse was busy in his room, and Karl had an idea. He couldn't speak, so he started spelling words by blinking at the nurse. One blink was an "a," three blinks was an "o," and so on.

"W-h-e-n-c-a-n-I-w-a-l-k?" Karl blinked out the words to the nurse. She put down what she was working on, sadness sweeping across her face as she gently said, "Didn't the doctors tell you? You'll never be able to walk again, Karl. I am so sorry." Her words hung in the room like a thick fog.

Karl could feel the tears rolling from the corners of his eyes and down into his ears. These were the only places he could still feel.

As the weight of her words sank in, it was as if Karl was under water once again, this time sinking very deep. The nurse came in close and wiped Karl's tears away as her own streamed down her cheeks.

Karl then slowly blinked his next message to her. "W-h-e-n-c-a-n-I-u-s-e-m-y-a-r-m-s?" The nurse, still sitting on his bed, searched for words. "Karl, I'm so very sorry. You hit the bottom so hard. You'll never be able to use your arms again either." She stroked Karl's hair, trying to offer some comfort, but it didn't help. Karl's neck injury had been so massive and his spinal cord was so damaged, the only things he would ever fully be able to use were his tongue, his eyes, and his mind.

Karl stayed in the hospital for months. He had stabilized, and the doctors and nurses switched their attention to helping him function in his new reality. During that time, a special vehicle was built so Karl could have mobility. Because Karl had the use of his tongue, a straw was attached to the steering mechanism. Karl uses small puffs of air and his tongue to steer forward and backward, to start, stop, and turn.

Karl was eventually discharged from the hospital. He had become used to the routine there and the relative comfort of learning his new life in a highly monitored environment. The discharge almost felt like he was being released to a prison as big as the whole world. He began figuring things out one by one all over again. The specialized steering unit was outfitted so Karl could answer the telephone, write emails, and do just about every other task the rest of us take for granted. Karl had to relearn how to navigate his entire life using just his tongue, his eyes, and his mind.

Karl wasn't a quitter. Even though his body had been wrecked, he still had the spirit of a fighter and a prankster. He took up the challenge with gusto. After graduating from high school, Karl went to college. He had adjusted to his new life but felt a growing vacuum deep inside of him. It wasn't just that he couldn't move any longer; he felt his whole life had lost any kind of trajectory. He didn't want his greatest achievements to be what he learned to do with a straw. He felt a growing need to somehow find more meaning and purpose than his life had offered even before his injuries.

During his freshman year at college, Karl met a couple of people who told him about a carpenter from Nazareth who had changed them. They were part of a campus group that got together every week, and they invited Karl to some of their meetings. What Karl found most compelling from where he sat was that this carpenter they talked about had navigated His entire life using only love.

The Bible talks a lot about our tongues, our eyes, and our

minds. It says we'll navigate much of our lives with them, just like Karl navigates his. Many of us have arms and feet we can move to help others, but we choose not to. We shy away from people we don't understand or who intimidate us because they're different from us. We have eyes to see people who are hurting, but we only watch because we're scared if we get closer, it will disrupt what we've spent a lifetime making orderly. We have minds to understand the depths of others' pain, but we just empathize without getting involved because we're scared of what might happen if we do. Karl lost the ability to use his arms and legs, but he learned to overlook this as an impediment. Many of us are limited by what we have but don't use. Karl didn't want to be limited by what he had but couldn't use. Being stripped of so many capabilities, he was forced to go deeper and find something worth the chase. Karl put his trust in Jesus. Karl was convinced after reading the claims Jesus had made that he could actually change the world using only his tongue and his eyes and his mind.

Karl and I went to law school together. We met on the first day of class. He was a hard guy to miss in the hallway with the machine he used to get around. He was stunningly kind and smart and loving. What was most striking about him, though, was he found a freedom in his life most of us are still looking for in ours.

Karl and I sat for the bar exam at the same time and he finished before me. You know why? He's got a fast tongue. Since passing the bar on his first try, Karl has been working at the attorney general's office. He chases bad guys for a living, running toward injustice with passion and purpose. His quick mind and even quicker tongue have proven to be more than enough for him to make his mark on the world, to do justice, and to express his love for God in many ways. Karl has had five cases go to California's supreme court. He won five times. Not only this, but he's had more than one hundred published decisions that have shaped the laws on criminal justice and victims' rights, affecting millions of people.

Karl's life is not unlike the story of a young boy with a few fish and some bread. Jesus tells us to bring what we have to Him, and He will make something amazing out of it. Karl just keeps bringing what he's got to Jesus. I think we should do the same; just keep bringing whatever you have to God and let Him decide what He'll do with it.

When I think about Karl's fateful dive, I think about how his body followed his head. He looked down to wave at the girls, and his body went where his eyes were looking. This is how we're all wired. Where we turn our heads is where we'll land with our lives. It happens all the time with careers or relationships or possessions. It doesn't matter whether it's comparison or distraction or escape that turns our heads—what we look at will be the difference between a great dive and a big disaster. Most of us won't break our necks when we look or leap wrong, but we may do something equally crippling in a different way.

We need to be careful where our minds dwell. Many of us

dwell on what other people are thinking of us. It's easy to do. But we can be so busy trying to get the approval of others that we forget who Jesus said we are. Here's the problem: when we're busy getting our validation from the people around us, we stop looking for it from God. You'll know this is happening to you when you go with what's popular rather than what's eternal, when you settle for what feels good right now rather than opting for what will make a good and lasting impact a decade from now. If we let our heads turn toward the shallow waters offered by wrong relationships, the rest of our lives will follow where our heads have gone. When we do, we'll crater instead of create, and we'll drown in the places where we ought to be swimming.

On our last day of law school, Karl said he was sending a car to pick up some friends and me. We climbed in, and the car took us to a field north of San Diego. We didn't know what had been planned for us, and a great deal of attention had been given to keeping the evening shrouded in secrecy. We guessed we were getting together with Karl to have a celebration picnic on the beach and to throw a Frisbee around a little. Instead, when we were far enough north to turn left to the beach, we turned inland and an open field came into view.

In the middle of the field stood a gigantic, colorful hot-air balloon a hundred feet tall with streamers hanging from the sides. A pilot standing in a wicker basket blasted flames into the canopy and the balloon tugged at the lines tethering it to the ground.

Next to the wicker basket was a guy in a wheelchair who had steered it there with a straw. Karl wanted to do something amazing for us that he would never have the chance to experience himself.

People who have developed a friendship with Jesus and are becoming love aren't immune to life's setbacks. They have just as many as everyone else. Sometimes I wonder if they have a few more, but I haven't tried to count. People like Karl have found something many of us are still looking for. He knows he's neither defined nor limited by his circumstances. He sees power in his brokenness and opportunities in the opposition he faces. Karl's not stuck trying to figure out why this thing happened to him; he's too busy celebrating other people's lives and making things happen for them. People like Karl don't think about what they've lost. They think about what they'll do with what they still have. And the answer is *much*.

In that field outside of San Diego, we stumbled our way into the hot air–balloon basket. The lines holding us to the ground were untied, and after a couple of loud flame blasts we began to float away. As we did, big things became small and close things seemed far away. The experience was probably not a lot different than what might happen when we get to heaven and look down on our lives, because there will be no impediments nor limiting beliefs blocking our view anymore. Karl had given us the gift of a new perspective. It was the kind of worldview Karl had found long before but we were just discovering through his beautiful life.

We looked over the edge of the basket as we were lifted into the sky and waved to Karl. He couldn't wave back, of course, but he didn't need to. Great love expressing itself in the world doesn't need any arm waving; it's always recognizable and leaves little doubt in the lives of the people it touches.

CHAPTER 14

Land the Plane

God doesn't give us all the details,
because He trusts us.

Each of us has a place that feels like heaven, a place where it's easier to sense God's creativity expressed in love and joy, mountains and streams. For my family and me, it's a lodge we built at the end of an inlet in British Columbia, Canada. It's a place where the waters of the Pacific are rimmed by eight-thousand-foot snow-capped mountains. A few times a year, killer whales bob slowly through the inlet and you can hear them exhale across the glassy water. Untouched cedar forests are filled with trees that were saplings before cars were invented. The Lodge is a dream more than twenty-two years in the making. It started with a couple of tents the first year, then eventually we added a lodge and surrounding buildings with enough beds for seventy people. It has become our place for restoration and adventure. God is somehow easier to find there.

But with all the beauty come some small inconveniences. There are no roads for one hundred miles in any direction. We make our own electricity off a glacier on the property, grow our own vegetables, and catch dinner in the ocean and rivers. Getting the things we need, like engine parts, is no small task. Taking a boat to this place is possible, but it's a long trip. So, when I stumbled on an old DeHavilland Beaver seaplane for sale, I knew it was the solution we needed. All I'd need to learn was how to fly it. What could possibly go wrong?

Beavers are guy planes. If they could make them out of beef jerky, they would. The nine-piston, 500-horsepower engine—called the "Wasp Junior" by the manufacturer—is junior to none and all steel and power. They stopped making these airplanes sixty years ago, so they're pretty frayed around the edges now. The way you know a Beaver engine is out of oil is when it stops leaking.

The fuselage has an old-world craftsmanship to it. It's not made from sheet metal or pre-fab fiberglass. It's pure tough, and looks like it could take some hits from heavy guns or bears or avalanches or preschool kids and keep going. It's the kind of plane Indiana Jones would fly out of a remote jungle. Actually, Harrison Ford owns a Beaver and in a couple of movies, this actually happened. A Beaver has pontoons because it's made to land on water instead of a runway. When we're at the Lodge, I usually fly out every week or two and fill it up with things we need—like ice cream and Pop Tarts—and fly back.

Going to the Lodge is something we count the days for in the Goff family. Every year as school winds down in late May, spring fever takes over on steroids. The house gets charged with planning and anticipation for the trek north for the summer. When our kids were in school, it was downright torturous. They'd be stuck in first-period English knowing a few weeks later they'd be skipping rocks next to hundred-foot waterfalls and foraging for dinner.

We try to get up to the Lodge a different way each year. Richard graduated from high school and we were looking for some adventure, so we bought some Harleys and Triumphs and rode motorcycles there. We started in Mexico and crossed North America, bottom to top. None of us had ever been on the highway with a motorcycle before. We figured we'd learn what we needed to know on the way. By the time we got to San Francisco, we could even change gears. Another year, Richard, who is infinitely winsome, led us on an amazing adventure as we fixed up a 1971 Volkswagen Bus. Richard drove it up to Canada, and he and Adam drove it back. Richard kept that bus for years and still leads us with creativity and laughter.

Adam was going into his senior year of high school. He was normally a great student, really disciplined and focused. But at that point, high school just felt kind of over to him. He had most of what he needed to get into college, and the last year felt like a punishingly slow victory lap.

One evening close to the start of the school year, I asked to see Adam's class list. He went up to his room and was there for a long time. When he came back downstairs to the kitchen table where I was sitting, he stared at his feet as he reluctantly handed it over. I looked at the list from top to bottom and laughed. "Where are the classes?" He tried to hold back a grin but didn't do a very good job.

His class list was ridiculous. I don't remember exactly, but I think he was the hall monitor for one period, cleaned erasers for another, had an art class, and was working in the school office the rest of the day. This was the schedule of a guy with his feet up on the handlebars and his fingers woven together behind his head.

Sure, I was sympathetic. Adam was beyond bored with school. Nothing really lit him up anymore. I remember the same thing happening to me in high school. Rather than coming down on Adam about his class list, we put our heads together and came up with a plan. What he needed was a challenge big enough to hold his attention for the year.

I had him sign up for a few real classes, and we got rid of all the other time fillers. For his senior year, Adam would leave school at noon each day and head to the airport to get his pilot's license. Instead of coasting through his last year of high school, he would ride it out at cruising altitude.

Sweet Maria thought Adam flying an airplane every day was a terrible idea, particularly when she heard he would be flying it alone after only a couple of weeks of lessons. I told Adam to think of his after-school program as a pass/fail class. You crash, you fail.

Adam would come home every day and tell us about what he learned. He would describe the cockpit and the preflight check-lists. His vocabulary was peppered with new terms like *pitch* and *yaw*. He was insistent about telling us the process for buckling the seatbelt in the airplane. I think he did this to show his mom he was taking his lessons seriously and wouldn't die. Our house wasn't just a home anymore; it was a Top Gun school. By the end of the year, Adam got a diploma, a pilot's license, and a leather jacket all in the space of a few days. He also got a seaplane rating so he could fly my Beaver.

There are thousands of remote mountain lakes in British Columbia. These emerald lakes are scattered everywhere, isolated between the steep granite walls of the surrounding mountains. Whenever I fly over them, I size them up and wonder if they would be big enough to land on.

For more than a decade, the boys and I had been eyeing one of these lakes. It freezes solid each winter and is covered by ten feet of snow, but by the end of the summer, the snow and ice melt away, leaving a jaw-dropping alpine lake behind. The lake isn't large. From the air, it looks like it's no more than a curbside puddle after a rainstorm. Each time we would fly over the lake, we would nudge one another and wonder out loud whether there was enough lake to land the Beaver—and if we did, would there be enough room to get back out again?

The entry point for the Beaver is a tight squeeze between two towering granite walls. If you make it through, the lake is at the bottom of a two-thousand-foot ravine. Getting there requires an aggressive descent. Each step requires total commitment because both the ravine and the deep bowl containing the lake are too cramped to turn around midway. Once you're in, there's no option but to land the plane and prepare for a new takeoff going the other direction. It's a round trip made of two one-way tickets.

One day, Adam and I were flying the Beaver back from a grocery run to town. As we passed over the lake, I looked over and asked, "What if we land in the lake today?" Adam laughed it off nervously.

"No, I'm serious. Let's do it!"

Adam stared at me for a long moment, wondering if I meant it. I took that as a yes and dipped the wing toward the lake and we started descending. The cockpit became charged with an intense mixture of fear and excitement.

We leveled the wings a few thousand feet over the lake and started the approach. The entry point was as narrow as it looked from the air. We were reaching the point where we couldn't turn around or pull out. I looked next to me, and Adam had a steely-eyed resolve as he looked through the windshield. We entered between the mountains and immediately things got much louder. The engine roar bounced off both granite walls and flooded the cockpit with noise. I looked out both side windows to get a visual of my orientation to the rock walls on either side. The wing was a safe but short distance from the granite wall on the right, and I was confident as we navigated this part of the approach. Next, we would descend to the lake.

As soon as we cleared the entrance, I pushed the controls forward. Before, we were looking at the mountains straight ahead. Now, we were looking mainly at the water as we flew the length of the lake. I was stunned by how beautiful it looked but quickly shook that off. No time for sightseeing. Adam's eyes were big enough to take it in for the both of us.

Even though we were making a sharp descent, we didn't have enough room to land the Beaver straight in. At the end of the lake, there was a widening of the rock walls just big enough for a final descending turn. It was a tight area to maneuver but was doable. I got as close as I could to the rock wall at the end of the lake and rolled the plane's wing one more time. We weren't perpendicular to the water, but it felt like it. I pushed the yoke all the way forward this time to descend the last four hundred feet to the lake.

Once you make that last turn, dropping the last few hundred feet needs to happen in a hurry but with a lot of care. If you land short, you hit the rocks; if you go too long, you hit the trees. If you've ever seen a pelican dive-bomb to catch a sardine, it was a lot like that but with more grace and less fish.

After going down the elevator pretty fast, we flattened our descent just a foot or two over the water, flared, and set the plane down. The pontoons skimmed across the calm alpine water and settled in. We slowed to a stop, and I cut the engine and unpeeled my hands from the controls.

Adam and I sat silently for a couple of seconds, staring out the front of the plane. Then we looked at each other and huge grins ripped across both of our faces.

"We did it! We landed in the lake!" We yelled into the silence as we high-fived in the cockpit. After all those years of looking and wondering if it could be done, we now had the answer.

But that was only half the equation. We still needed the answer to the other half. Was there enough lake for us to get out? I could see Adam's mind grinding out the possibilities and what he would do. So I turned to look at him.

"Okay, Adam, *you* fly us out of here."

He shook his head violently, like a Labrador retriever with water in its ears.

"No way." He had a stern look to him, like he meant business. But I did too.

While he was protesting, I unbuckled myself, got out of the pilot's seat, and moved to a back passenger seat to make way for the new pilot. There was only one other place to sit, so Adam snapped into the pilot's seat, gripped the controls, and just stared. It was game on.

Adam taxied the plane all the way back to the weeds at the far end of the lake. He was setting up the plane like a sprinter putting his feet into the starting blocks.

A Beaver needs to be going fifty-two miles an hour before it will lift off the water. If you try to take off when you're going only forty-eight miles an hour, the pontoon floats will dig into the water and slow you down, and you'll run out of lake and hit the trees. If you wait until you're going seventy miles per hour, you'll run out of lake and hit the trees. Adam knew the stakes, and I reminded him to keep his eye on the speed because what he did would determine where we'd be spending the next few days.

We would need every inch of lake to get up and over the trees at the far end. Sometimes prayers are spoken, and other times they are said in our actions. Adam put his hands on the controls and threw in all the throttle. I said, "Amen."

I had one eye on the speedometer as the plane picked up speed. Adam got us to thirty and then forty miles per hour. The plane skipped across the surface like a ski boat. He kept increasing the speed while the trees at the other end kept getting bigger in the windshield. When the plane passed fifty-two miles per hour, I started anticipating liftoff. Adam knew what to do to get us off the water.

Adam pulled back before we ran out of lake, and we cleared the tops of the trees as we sailed out of the canyon.

Adam let out a big yelp, and I was woohoo-ing. I was going to give him a chest bump but figured we'd crash, so I didn't. The lake was disappearing behind us as we flew back toward the Lodge, all grins. I bet Adam was working on the story we would tell everybody when we got there.

I turned to Adam again and said, "Okay, turn the plane around and let's see if you can land us back in the lake." Adam started shaking his head again so hard I thought it might fall off. We had a good enough story, right? Then I saw him mentally switch, and he started to turn the plane.

When Adam entered the canyon, I didn't say anything.

When he started descending into the canyon, I didn't say anything.

When he made his turn at the wide spot at the end of the lake, he nailed it. I didn't say anything.

As we made the final descent toward the lake, Adam threw the yoke forward. We were still fifty feet off the water when he flew past where I had landed previously. I didn't say anything.

Adam landed the plane like a boss, and we came to a stop. Adam had flown into that canyon as an eighteen-year-old, but when the Beaver touched down on the water he looked thirty-five. I looked like I was a hundred and twenty.

The whole time all of this was happening, I was thinking this: *Land. The. Plane.*

God isn't always leading us to the safest route forward but to the one where we'll grow the most. I knew Adam well enough to know he could land the plane. I'd seen him do it a hundred times in more open waters. I had already told him everything I knew about it. He didn't need any more instructions; he just needed to see I believed in him enough to let him do it. He didn't need more words or to know what they meant in Greek or Hebrew. He just needed an opportunity.

The people who have shaped my faith the most did the same for me. They didn't try to teach me anything; they let me know they trusted me. And that taught me everything. Those moments are forever etched into who I am. I think God does the same with us.

I've heard a lot of people say they wish they could hear from God about this or that. Maybe they mean they want to hear His audible voice. I'm not sure. I don't think literally hearing something is what most of us are after. What we actually want is that extra nudge of confidence from God and the opportunity to move forward courageously to do those things we already know how to do. What a shame it would be if we were waiting for God to *say* something while He's been waiting on us to *do* something. He speaks to me the loudest on the way. Simply put, if we want more faith, we need to do more stuff.

Part of me really understands people's hesitation. There have been times when I wanted to hear God's voice—particularly, when something really big mattered to me. The sad truth is, I'm often making too much racket to hear Him. He won't try to shout over all the noise in our lives to get our attention. He speaks most clearly in the stillness desperation brings.

I've also come to see the purpose and beauty in God's silence. It's like He's telling me He knows my heart's desires and what I'm thinking. He knows what He's taught me. He's seen when I've succeeded and when I've failed. From His point of view, that all rolls up into an unspoken whisper from Him I can almost hear saying, "You've got this." His biggest priority isn't removing failure as an option but reminding me He loves me as I try. There's a verse in the Bible that says, "Do not despise these small beginnings." I love that. It's a reminder to me God doesn't just value the big endeavors that work and He isn't afraid we'll fail; instead, He delights in our attempts.

God knows we won't do everything picture-perfect either. If we're being honest, our mess-ups outnumber our successes, probably by a wide margin. More than once, I've been a little too close to the rocks and a little out of position. I've come in a little hot, gone a little long, or fallen a little short in the things I've attempted.

But God hasn't been shouting instructions to me as I've made mistakes because He doesn't need to. His silence isn't indifference; it's engagement. He isn't quiet because He's run out of things to say or is scared about the outcome. It's because He already believes in me, just as much as He knows the outcome. He already believes in you too. He's so confident we already know what to do next that He's willing to be silent even when we ask for His voice. He doesn't care as much as we do whether we perform perfectly or not. He just wants us to be His while we do it.

Most of us don't need more instructions; we simply need someone who believes in us. If we're fortunate, God will surround us with friends who know us so well they've stopped trying to control our conduct with endless instructions and instead trust that God is at work in our lives, even if He's doing things we don't yet understand.

It's perfectly normal and okay to feel afraid and confused and stationary. It happens to all of us at one time or another. We shouldn't be surprised when we don't understand what a God who says He surpasses all understanding is doing. God doesn't want us to get stuck scratching our heads or overanalyzing our circumstances. He doesn't send in all the plays to get us out of our funk, and He doesn't carpet-bomb us with instructions about what to do next. Instead, He continues to be *with* us. He's not entirely silent when He is either. He's sent us books about Him and has included a lot of letters, and He's sent us friends too. He's given us successes and failures—plenty of both. He's written things on our hearts like love and grace and patience and compassion so we can write those things on the hearts of our friends. We're God's calligraphy. He doesn't do this so our words will look better, but because He sees the beauty in our lives.

When we dream up something where the outcome seems uncertain and we don't hear God's voice, what if God isn't saying anything to us because He's already said it? Like my time with Adam flying into the lake, I can picture God sitting beside each of us, not confused or afraid but confident we have all the information we need. We may not have had experience with the circumstances we're presently facing, but He's allowed us to experience a lifetime of other things to prepare us for what is coming next.

He knows that without risk we can't grow. God didn't promise us a safe life. Instead, He said He would give us a dangerous, courageous, and purposeful one if we'll take Him at His word and stay engaged. Sometimes God is confidently quiet. He doesn't give us more explanations. He knows we don't need more words of instruction. The moment we take even a tiny shuffle forward, what God is already thinking about us is this: *I love you. You've got this. You know enough.*

What big idea do you have that you've not pursued because you didn't know if it would work? Who have you wanted to reach out to in love but were afraid you'd be rejected? Who has broken your heart? Who took advantage of you in a business deal? Who misunderstood you? Who do you need to forgive? Now's your time. Don't wait any longer. You know what to do. You've got this. You know enough.

Go land the plane.

CHAPTER 15

A Welcome from Walter

What we do with our love will become
the conversations we have with God.

I have a friend named Walter. After the government was over-
thrown in his country, he escaped from jail in a hail of bullets
and fled to the United States for safety. Now Walter helps people
resettle here after they've been forced from their homes in other
countries. Many of them arrive at airports in the United States
straight from United Nations refugee camps overseas. They step
off the plane having experienced years of hunger and thirst, dis-
placement, and fear. Confused. Scared. Lonely. They come as
strangers to this new place. They don't stop at baggage claim for
luggage, because they have no clothes. Nor do they have any idea
who they'll meet, where they'll live, or what they'll do once they
arrive. They're easy to spot when they step off the plane, because
most still have UN tags dangling from lanyards around their necks.

After getting off the plane, America's newest guests walk

awkwardly and tentatively toward the arrival terminal, busier people edging by them in the halls. Anxiety grows on their faces with each step. Then everything changes for them when they see Walter standing at the gate with his huge smile and his arms stretched wide, reaching out toward them. Walter welcomes these beautiful people to their new lives. He treats them as if they were Jesus Himself—because Walter knows Jesus, and Jesus said the way Walter treats these people is the way he's treating Him.

Walter let me come along with him to the airport to greet some arriving refugees. I didn't know what to bring with me, so I brought a dozen helium balloons. Balloons are my go-to for everything when I don't know what to bring. I take them to birthday parties, job interviews, dentist appointments, bar exams, to the gym—everywhere except scuba diving. Balloons are an internationally understood code for celebration, joy, welcome, acceptance, and love.

I think heaven might be a little like the greeting Walter gives to the refugees he meets at the airport. A celebration, a homecoming. None of us will need any luggage either. (I'm expecting plenty of balloons when I get there; I can't lie.) From what I've read, we'll get a chance to meet Jesus and we'll have a discussion with Him. It's not the kind of discussion someone has when they get sent to the principal at school. It will be more of an uncovering, a revealing of what we didn't understand during our lives. For most of us, I bet it will involve a tremendous unlearning of many of the things we thought we were certain of.

Jesus referred to two groups. He called them sheep and goats when He talked about the discussion we'll have with Him, but He meant you and me. He said we'll talk about how we treated the people we came across during our lives and whether we treated them as if they were Him. These are people like the ones Walter greets at the airport—the hungry, the thirsty, the strangers. People who are sick or don't have clothes. People under bridges and in jail cells. Jesus told His friends we'll all hear about the times when we saw Him during our lives but didn't recognize Him and the couple of times we did.

I've got a long list of questions I want to talk to God about when we meet. For instance, I'd like to know how God decided where to put the waterfalls in Yosemite. Have you seen them? They're huge and majestic. And I want to know about Half Dome too—where's the other half? Sadly, it seems none of the questions on my list are the things Jesus will want to discuss with me. Jesus won't want to talk about our elections or impeachments, who got the rose from a bachelor, or who got the boot from a boss. What it seems He'll care about most is how we treated the people on the fringes of our lives. He'll want to talk about whether we gave them a hug or some much-needed help. All of this because He said if we did kind things for the lonely and hurting and isolated in the world we were really doing it for Him.

I can hear how the discussion with the first group who did the right things but didn't know it was Jesus might go down.

"Wait. Really? That was you? No way! The guy with all the tattooed cuss words? The hooker? That guy in jail? The kid in Uganda? The lawyer? The schoolteacher? The politician?" "We didn't know it was You. We just decided we'd love people the way You said to."

The second group will be just as surprised by what they hear Jesus say. This group didn't intend to be mean or uncaring. They are a lot like you and me in this way. I'm sure they would have been more than willing to help Jesus if He'd asked them, but when the hungry or thirsty or sick or strange people came along, or when people without clothes came by, they didn't know what to do, so they didn't do anything.

It wasn't that they disagreed with Jesus or folded their arms and refused to help. Their mistake was simple. In fact, it's the one I make almost every day; they just didn't recognize these people were actually Jesus. These people didn't dress like Him or talk like Him or act like Him. In fact, the opposite was true. They lived in a way and did things that were quite opposite of how Jesus lived. Some of the things they did landed them in jail or left them in perilous positions. Jesus knew this, and He said if we wanted to be with Him, we'd stop playing it safe and go talk *to* them instead of talking *about* them.

I've lived most of my life as a second-group guy. I have simply been too busy and too good at keeping my distance from people I don't understand to know what they really needed. Sure, I noticed them, but I just wasn't close enough to recognize it wasn't just hurting, lonely people I was passing by—it was Jesus I was avoiding. Sadly, sometimes I only pretend to care for people who are hurting. The way I know this is simple—I don't do anything to help them. I'll say I am too busy to help someone in need when it isn't time

I lack; it's compassion. In short, I settle for merely hoping rather than actually helping.

We all know people like Walter. People who seem to have all the time in the world for other people. The reason is simple. Walter thinks every needy person he meets is Jesus. People who are becoming love make this look easy.

As a father, I know if someone wants to do something nice for me, they do it for my kids. Good fathers are like that. When someone does something terrific for my kids, they don't even need to tell me. Fathers always seem to find out. Mothers know before it even happens. I bet that's how God feels too. Jesus said when we give away love freely to one another and meet the needs of poor and needy and isolated and hurting people, we're actually doing it for Him. Even when we don't know we are. He said if we wanted to do something nice for God, we'd do it for His kids. And we don't need to make a big deal out of it either. He'll find out. Good Fathers do.

I've met a lot of people who say they're waiting for God to give them a "plan" for their lives. They talk about this "plan" like it's a treasure map God has folded up in His back pocket. Only pirates have those. People who want a reason to delay often wait for plans. People who are becoming love don't. It's almost as if Jesus knew we'd invent excuses under the guise of waiting for His "plan," so He made it simple for us. He said His plan for all of us was to love Him and then find people who are hungry or thirsty or who feel like strangers or are sick or don't have clothes or are in prison or creep us out or are our enemies and go love them just like they were Him.

Game. Set. Match. We can stop looking for another plan—that's it.

Instead of just agreeing with Jesus, I started looking around my life for the kind of people Jesus said we'd be talking about when we finally meet Him on the other side of heaven's threshold. I was kind of hoping I could find just one guy who was hungry and thirsty and sick and strange and naked and in jail. This way I could get it all done at once. It doesn't work that way, though. I've found out it's everybody. It's all of us, in one way or another. It's me. It's you. It's the person next to you at the coffee shop right now. I know it's hard to believe, but they're Jesus—even the ones who look and act so differently than He did.

Don't make this more complicated than it is. Just start. Go find someone who is hungry right now and do something about it. I've heard lots of people say that giving the poor a fishing pole is better than giving them a meal, but I don't see them giving away many fish *or* poles.

We have a fast-food place called In-N-Out Burger near our home. I'll buy twenty burgers and then drive around town and ask people I meet if they're hungry. If they are, I hook them up with a hamburger. I don't write little messages on the wrapper like "Jesus loves you . . ." If you've ever had a Double-Double burger, you *know* He loves you!

Find strange people and welcome them into your life. You may have a whole family full of them already; no one will even notice. Keep water bottles in your car and find thirsty people. Go to a hospital and find sick people and give away love and Band-Aids and maybe one of your kidneys. Naked people are a little harder to find, but we have a nude beach not far away. I stand at the top of the cliff and throw socks over the edge. Here's the point: Don't just agree with Jesus. Go visit jails and make a couple of friends there. You don't even need to commit a felony to get in. Just ask the warden.

Do these things and you'll not only find your faith again; you'll find Jesus. Even better, you'll have plenty of things to talk to Him about for eternity in heaven. That's the plan.

CHAPTER 16

What Grace Costs

Grace doesn't cost as much as I thought.

These days I get lots of telephone calls because I left my cell number in the back of almost a million copies of my last book, *Love Does*. Jesus was available to everyone, and I am reminded of the power of engaging strangers as I field dozens of calls from them daily. People don't follow vision; they follow availability. I don't send people to voice mail anymore. Try it for a week. Loving people the way Jesus did means living a life filled with constant interruptions. Take the calls. Interrupt your days. Be excessively available, and you'll be just like Jesus.

There's a kid who calls me every three weeks and cusses at me. I'm a lawyer and thought I'd heard all the bad words before. Evidently there are some new ones because he's unloaded quite a few on me. The funny thing is we've never gotten to what he's mad about. Each time before he hangs up, I tell him, "I'll always take your call." Here's why: I don't want him to climb a tower with a rifle or say these things to someone who just walked out of a biker bar. They'll kill him.

I've got the young man tagged on caller ID as "Vulgar Kid" because I need to brace myself each time before I get an earful from him. Is it fair he says mean things to me? Of course not. But here's what's changing in me: I don't want what's fair anymore. I want to be like Jesus. It's a distinction worth making.

One day, I was in my office with a person who had some legal problems. The phone rang, and I explained to the person who was with me I never send people to voice mail. I excused myself and answered my phone. I was disappointed to hear a recording on the other end.

"Hello, you have a call from . . ."

I hung up. I didn't need any cooking knives or spot remover or the investment opportunity I was sure the recorded telemarketer was selling. I rejoined my meeting and started back in the conversation where I had left off.

A few minutes later, the phone rang again. A little embarrassed, I excused myself for this next interruption, picked up the phone, and got the same recording.

"Hello, you have a call from . . ."

I figured this time I'd just listen to the end of the recording and press the button telling them not to call me anymore. The recorded message continued, "You have a call from the Sacramento State Penitentiary. Press #5 for your call and you will be charged $9.95 on your phone bill." Wait, what? I immediately pressed #5 several times. I wanted to see who I'd end up with. Who wouldn't, right?

My pride had the conversation entirely figured out before it even started. No doubt, there was some guy who had been thrown in jail in Sacramento. I guessed someone probably gave him *Love Does* to read while he was locked up, and he was probably calling me to tell me he had read the book and what a great guy I was. I felt myself puff up with undeserved pride as someone picked up the line at the other end.

"Hello, this is Bob," I said, as I waited for the accolades to start flowing. There was a pause. And then a man's stern voice broke through.

"Where's Shanice?"

Shoot. He wasn't even calling for me. It was a wrong number. Deflated, I told the fellow Shanice wasn't here. It was just me, Bob. He gave a disappointed humph and hung up.

I laughed at myself and my stupid pride and got back into my legal conversation. Then the phone rang again.

"Hello, you have a call from . . . you will be charged $9.95 . . ." I pressed #5.

"Hi, this is Bob."

"Will you call Shanice for me?" said the inmate.

I started laughing. "Buddy, I'd love to help you, but I'm not sure how I could even do that for you." Then I remembered I could press a button on my phone and conference her into the call.

"Let me try to patch her in. What's her number?" He gave it to me, and I immediately understood how he'd misdialed me in the first place. Her number was almost identical to the number in the back of *Love Does*.

I dialed the number. It rang a couple of times before someone picked it up, but it wasn't Shanice. It was a guy. I wasn't trying to listen in, but it was a conference call, so I was already on the line. "Where's Shanice?" my jail friend asked. "She's with me now," the other guy grunted, and then he hung up.

I was so sad for my new friend in jail, but I could also understand how complicated relationships can be and why people move on with their lives when someone they loved is away in jail for a long time. I hung up the phone, shook my head, and went back to work.

And then the phone rang again.

"Hello, you have a call from . . ." I pressed #5.

"Will you call my mother?"

I laughed. It was like I was this guy's concierge. "You bet, friend. What's her number?" I said, amused at how my day was turning out. I dialed the number he gave me.

The phone rang a couple of times, and while it was still just the two of us on the line, I told him I thought it was great he was calling his mom. On the fifth ring, his mother answered. They said a few things to each other, then my new friend said, "Mom, I just wanted to call to let you know that I love you." She didn't say anything in response. She hung up on him.

I welled up. It was just my jail friend and me on the phone again. I didn't know what to say, so I offered, "Man, I'm so sorry that happened. That's got to hurt." I was thinking perhaps he had tried to reach his girlfriend or mom because he was going to ask them for help, so I offered, "Hey, what is it that you need, anyway?"

There was another pause as if he were deciding whether he trusted me enough to ask. Then my new friend sheepishly said,

"I need a bracelet." I had thought of a long list of things he might have asked me for—a cake with a hacksaw in it, an alibi, breath mints—but I wouldn't have put money on him asking me for a bracelet.

"You want to wear a bracelet?" I asked naively as I tried to visualize this guy sporting a gold wristband covered in sequins as he bench-pressed 350 pounds in the prison yard.

"No, no. I've been in jail for four years and I've qualified to be released with an ankle bracelet. I just need to pay for it." For those who are unfamiliar, an ankle bracelet is what the police put on people they want to keep track of as a condition of their release. Without missing a beat, I said, "Buddy, I'll buy it for you. What color do you want?" We both laughed, and he said they didn't come with colors, just locks.

The next day I got in touch with the prison so I could buy this guy an ankle bracelet. They told me how much it cost. I gasped and reached for my chest. I had the guy tell me the number again because I thought I had misheard him the first time. I had no idea how much it cost to LoJack a felon. But I made a promise, so I wrote the check. I assume the guy got his bracelet because the prison said they released him a few days later. I haven't heard from him since, but I know he's got my number.

Here's the thing: we don't need to put ankle bracelets on all the good things we do for God like we're trying to keep track of them. In fact, He said to do just the opposite. Jesus talked about not letting one of your hands even know what the other is up to. There are probably a number of reasons He gave this metaphor, but among them is when we do things for the poor or the sick or strange or naked or those in jail, He already knows all about it because it's Him.

When I was in elementary school, we put on the classic play *Peter Pan*. I tried out for the role of Peter, but I couldn't sing or dance or fly so I didn't get it. (Actually, I *can* fly, but don't tell anyone.) I did get a part, though. My official title was Tree #4. I had no lines. I didn't even get a name, like maple or birch or oak. My role was to just stand there, hold my arms out above my shoulders, wiggle my fingers, and look like a tree. There was no mention of my name in the program they handed out. There were no bouquets of roses given to me on opening or closing night. I didn't get a backstage room with a star or leaf on the door, and there was no cast party celebrating my performance. You know what? I loved it! Here's why: I knew what was needed; my role was clear and it wasn't too complicated. In short, I knew what I was there to do. Many of us don't.

Something changes for many of us after we leave elementary school. We try to make ourselves the hero or the victim of every story. Something goes wrong and we want to be the victim; something goes right and we want to make ourselves the hero. It doesn't seem to matter which it is as long as we make it all about us. But if we make everything about us, it'll never be about Jesus. What I'm coming to realize is we're not the heroes and we're not the victims of all the stories happening around us. We're just Tree #4.

I wasn't the hero for getting the guy an ankle bracelet. I wasn't the victim because it cost me a bundle. I was just doing the kind of thing Jesus said people who are trying to become love do. I was just being Tree #4 in this jail guy's life.

Even when we do it right, often we don't land it right. Here's what I mean: Jesus knew some of us would be tempted to tell everyone who would listen about all the things we'd done. He talked about religious people standing on street corners, but He was really talking about guys like me. Maybe He was talking about you too. He said if we made a big deal about what we'd done now, hoping to get someone to clap, we would have had our reward. We don't need to be the hero in everyone's story. Jesus already landed that part. When you do something for Jesus while He appears to be hungry or sick or thirsty or strange or naked or in jail, don't mess it up by making a big deal out of it. I once heard someone say, "If you want applause, join the circus." If you want to talk about it with Jesus forever, keep it quiet.

When I told Sweet Maria about my jail friend, she thought I was nuts. Who knows, she's probably right. We both laughed at the thought we'd come home one day soon and see this guy wearing an ankle bracelet, walking down the street and carrying our flat screen. I kind of hope he doesn't, but it'll be a great story if he does. It should be the same for you. Go ahead and risk it. You're just Tree #4. You don't need a bunch of lines; Jesus is in the lead role, and He's got it handled. All you need are a couple of arms to hold up in the air like branches and a few fingers to wiggle.

I'm guessing my friend from jail went on to do terrific things with his life, but even if he didn't, I did, and it was because of what I learned from him. He gave me one more thing to talk to Jesus about. Jesus doesn't need our help with the hungry or thirsty or sick or strange or naked or people in jails. I know this, because I asked Him. He wants our hearts. He lets us participate, if we're willing, so we'll learn more about how He feels about us and how He feels about the people we may have been avoiding.

There's an amazing chaplain and a group of guys in a prison in Michigan and another in Minnesota who teach me something about love every month or two. We exchange letters, and I've gone to visit them. Another group of prisoners started their own "Bible Doing" group. Many of them are in for life. They racked their minds about what they could do for others while imprisoned. They wiggled their fingers and used what they had. For $1.10 they can buy pairs of jail socks from the commissary. They mail them to me, and I've been giving them away for these guys. We may not be able to walk in their shoes, but we can walk in their socks.

I think these guys understand a lot more about what Jesus was talking about than I ever have. Jesus' invitation to us wasn't complicated. He said to go find people who are hurting and lonely and isolated—the ones who look wrong or did wrong—and learn from them what your faith is all about. Did the people in our jails make big mistakes? You bet. Is it easy to see their biggest failures? Of course. I'm not sure why Jesus said we should visit people who had failed big like my friend with the bracelet, but I wonder if it's because He knew we'd fail too.

When we get to heaven, I would have thought Jesus would want to talk about our terrific organizations or what nice people we were or the positions we held. Maybe these things will come up, but I doubt it. Instead, He said He will want to know how we treated the ones who had failed the worst.

I get dozens of calls these days from jails from all over the country, and I never refuse them. I think the prisoners are passing a *Love Does* book from cell to cell. Each time I take a call, I get a charge on my phone bill for $9.95. I don't take the calls because I'm looking for new friends. I do it because Jesus said we were supposed to, and I came to play, not to watch.

In *The Cost of Discipleship*, Dietrich Bonhoeffer famously said we make grace cost too little. I once heard my friend Mike Foster say we make grace cost too much. Honestly, I don't know which it is. Maybe both these guys are right. I haven't really tried to figure out what grace costs. But someday I know I'll get to talk to Jesus about it, and my guess is He'll tell me grace costs about $9.95.

CHAPTER 17

My Bucket

How is your life working for
the people around you?

I've been asked quite a few times how my life is working for me. It's a fair question, I suppose. More than just small talk, what my friends *really* want to know is how things are going for me. I think a better question to ask is, *How is your life working for the people around you?* Because if our lives aren't working for the people around us, our lives aren't working for us.

I have a friend whose home got toilet-papered. It was an ecological disaster, kind of like the Charmin version of the *Exxon Valdez*. It was really an unbelievable job. Hundreds of rolls of toilet paper had been spread over the lawn and the shrubs. Someone must have been the quarterback for the local high school football team, because there were toilet-paper streamers hanging a hundred feet long from the branches of the huge pine tree.

I wondered how my friend would get the highest streamers

down from the tree, and I learned a short time later he got a book of matches and lit the end of one of the long toilet-paper strands. Bad idea. It was like a fuse. The flame leapfrogged up the toilet paper, catching every intersecting strand on fire along the way. Within seconds, parts of the tree had caught fire. One of the branches fell on the neighbor's garage roof, which was three feet deep in pine needles from the tree, and it caught on fire. My friend's life was not working for the people around him.

How's your life working for the people who are closest to you?

I'm always in a hurry. I put on my socks two at a time. I lace up my tennis shoes while I run to save a couple of minutes. I order sushi at restaurants so I don't have to wait for them to cook the fish—and I don't even like sushi. When I'm not in a hurry, I spend my time being impatient. It's so extreme, sometimes I think I make coffee nervous.

While living my life this way has been working out great for me, I started to wonder how it was working for the people around me. So I asked them. Do you know what I found out? My impatience was driving them nuts.

A few weeks after I asked the question, I found a beautiful kids' book that changed everything for me. It was a book about buckets, and its premise was simple: we will become in our lives what we put in our buckets. I knew I needed to fill mine with patience.

I decided to put the book to the test, so I went to a hardware store and bought a metal bucket. I carried it with me everywhere for three weeks as an experiment. The bucket was made of galvanized aluminum and had a wire handle. I looked like a dairy farmer. I took my bucket with me in cars, on sailboats, in subways—everywhere. People on airplanes would ask if I had a bladder problem. "Actually," I'd say jokingly, "I do." But then I would say, "I have an even bigger problem. I'm *really* impatient." I let them know how I use the bucket as a reminder to fill my life with patience every day.

If we fill our buckets with a bunch of business deals, we'll turn into businesspeople. If we fill them with arguments, we'll become lawyers. If we fill them with a critical spirit, we'll become cynics. If we fill them with joy, we'll experience tremendous happiness. I believed in the concept behind the bucket so wholeheartedly, I filled my bucket with sprinkled doughnuts one day just to see what would happen to me.

Here's the simple message Jesus has for us: if we fill our buckets with love, we can actually become love.

I have a friend named Randy Phillips. He is an amazing guy who pastors an even more amazing church called LifeAustin. He also has a band called Phillips, Craig and Dean. I know it sounds like a law firm, but it's not. Randy asked me to come speak at his church one Sunday. He had called me almost a year in advance and gave me the date for the Sunday service. I jumped at the chance to be with Randy. What I didn't realize until the weekend finally arrived was the date he picked was Super Bowl Sunday. I don't watch much football during the season—I'm too impatient. But I love watching the Super Bowl. Actually, what I really love is being with Sweet

Maria and eating nachos. The Super Bowl gives me the excuse I need to do both.

I don't spend very many nights away from Sweet Maria. It happens from time to time and on overseas trips. The rest of the time, she usually drops me off at the airport each morning at 5:30. She never asks me where I'm going, and I never think to tell her. I'll usually go somewhere for the day and then I fly back home for a late supper. When someone asks her where I am, she always says the same thing, "He's on his way home," because I always am. There are nights I can't make it back, of course. We don't feel bad about it when it happens; we just try to have fewer of them.

I'm a pretty energetic person, so traveling and being around a lot of people works for me. What works for Sweet Maria, however, is to have me home. Because she is there, being home works pretty great for me too. So I don't think of all of the reasons I'm not going to be home; I just get there. I'll fly from Atlanta to San Diego for supper and back to the East Coast the next day. I've been doing this for years. I spent over twenty years commuting from San Diego to Seattle each morning, and I would make it back home for supper at night. Our kids were in junior high school before they knew. When they figured it out, they said, "Dad, you said you worked downtown."

"I do," I answered with a grin. They never asked me which city.

I'm not trying to be efficient in the way I love Sweet Maria and our kids; I'm trying to be present. There's a big difference between the two. One thing I've learned from Jesus is extravagant love is never wasted. Yours won't be either if you keep running home.

When I finished speaking at the last of several services at

Randy's church, I jumped into my rental car and bolted for the airport to get home for the last couple of plays of the Super Bowl. It was going to be tight, like usual. When I got to the rental-car return lot, there were a couple of lines with an attendant at the front of each. I chose my line and began waiting. Nothing happened for several minutes, so I craned my neck out the window to see what was the holdup. At the front of this line, an attendant was staring into the air as if he were trying to remember the words to a Rolling Stones song. I jiggled my foot on the brake impatiently. I tapped my fingers on the dashboard. After five minutes, I let out an audible, exasperated, "Really?" into my empty car. All the while, the line next to me was moving along just fine. I was more than a little peeved, I can't deny, as the cold realization sunk in. I got "that guy."

You know the one I'm talking about. The only gears he seemed to have were slow, stop, and reverse. I sat in my rental car, fingers still drumming on the steering wheel, waiting for him to gain consciousness. The car in front of me started to inch forward, but then it happened again. Entire seasons changed while I waited. I inched forward again. I was at the height of my frustration when I noticed my bucket in the passenger seat. I had completely forgotten about it.

"Fill it with patience," I said to myself over and over. "Fill it with patience." Finally, the attendant slowly lumbered toward me. I've seen glaciers move faster. He opened the door slowly and asked, "How was your rental-car experience?"

In the old days, I would have just clocked him with my bucket or made a wisecrack to let him know what a lousy job he was doing and how he had made me miss my flight.

Something different was going on inside me this time, though. For twenty-five minutes, I had done my best to fill my bucket with patience. This time, instead of making the snarky remark that easily came to mind, I said to the guy as I got out of my car, "I had a great time. The car was awesome. You're awesome. Airplanes are awesome. Life is awesome. I hope you have a great day." I didn't even recognize myself. It was like a ventriloquist had his hand up my shirt and was making my mouth move and was saying things for me. This certainly didn't sound like the old version of Bob talking. And you know what? It wasn't. It was a bucket filled with patience doing the talking.

I had missed my plane—by a lot. I got out of the car with my bucket and started walking to the terminal to book a new flight. I had walked halfway across the parking lot when the rental-car guy came running up from behind me and put his hand on my shoulder. A little winded, he said to me, "Hey, I just want you to know"—he paused to catch his breath before continuing—"that was a great sermon you gave at church."

You were there? I thought as I held back a gasp.

Oh man, if he only knew what was going on in my head while I was sitting in line before I remembered my bucket in the passenger seat.

We can pretend to have all the game we want to up on stage, in the pulpit, on the field, at work, or in our faith communities. But it's how we engage with the rental-car attendant or the grocery bagger or the bank teller or the person who puts on the car tires that lets everybody know where we really are with Jesus. I still get it wrong more than I get it right, but I was so grateful I had filled my bucket with the right stuff that day. All the words and emotions that otherwise would have spewed out of me would have shattered this guy and shown me for the impatient, selfish guy I'm still trying to put on the bus.

People will figure out what we really believe by seeing what we actually do. Everybody has a plan, but God is looking for people who know their purpose. As often as I try to make it look otherwise, most of the time I make everything about me. I make it about my schedule and my timing, how I'm feeling and how big of a hurry I'm in. Kind of like Paul in the Bible, I talk a good game, but I find myself doing exactly what I said I wouldn't do and not doing what I said I would do.

It's taken some time, but I'm starting to act like my purpose is to love God and to love the people around me the way Jesus loved the people around Him. As much as I'd like to make it more complicated and have more steps so I can find some cover for my inaction, it's really that simple. Loving my neighbors, even when they're the punishingly slow rental-car return guy, means I have to find a new way to engage them. To pull this off, I need to do it with an unreasonable amount of patience and kindness and understanding.

We all encounter difficulties. It's what we do next that defines us. During the times when I'm confused, my feelings have been hurt, or I'm exhausted or frustrated, I'm learning how to fill my bucket with love. People don't grow where they're planted; they grow where they're loved. Knowing things about the Bible is terrific. But I'd trade in a dozen Bible studies for a bucket full of acceptance—and truth be told, so would everyone around us.

While unloading on the rental guy the way I wanted to at

first might have worked for me for a few moments as I let off some steam, the conversation wouldn't have worked for him. Because I had been filling my bucket with patience, I'm sure I had the conversation I should have had with the rental-car guy that day. As a result, I let loose a lot of grace into the world. It's this simple and that difficult. The guy who is up in front at church needs to be the same guy in the back of the rental-car line. If you can't do that, either stop driving or get off the stage. Bringing those two different people together is going to take a whole lifetime—and a pretty big bucket.

My daughter, Lindsey, is a teacher. One year, when she was teaching kindergarten, she told me she was working on report cards. Lindsey didn't give As and Bs and Cs like I was used to in school. She gave the students different letters. For example, an "M" means they mastered the curriculum. A "G" means they were at grade level. My favorite grade, by far, was for the students who hadn't quite wrapped their minds around an idea. Those kids got an "N." Do you know what that stands for? "Not yet." Isn't that beautiful?

Jesus doesn't give any of us grades, and I'm grateful for that. He's the only one who ever loved people perfectly. None of us will ever get love and kindness or sacrifice entirely right. We're all just doing the best we can. While I've never tried to grade my faith, if I did, I think there would be quite a few areas where I'd give myself an "N." As much as I wish it were otherwise, I'm just not quite there yet.

What's sad is I'm not quite there on a number of the things Jesus said were the most important things to Him. For example, I get an "N" when it comes to loving the people who are well intentioned but make following Jesus feel like it's a homework assignment to be completed during weekend detention rather than a banquet with Him. I'm not quite there with people who push others away from Jesus because of their behavior, rather than drawing them in with love. This includes the ones who expect to meet people at the finish line rather than realizing we're all at the starting line in our faith. I'm just not quite there yet in the way I deal with people who have frustrated me or who slow me down. I also get an "N" for being as loving and accepting of people I disagree with as God wants me to be.

I don't love God with my whole heart and soul and mind yet like He asked me to. I think I do, but then I see how I treat people who are different than me and it often looks like a guy who's looking for a good deal in his faith, rather than a guy who's sold out to it. All of this said, God doesn't measure things the way we do and He doesn't grade us on a curve.

The first step is to realize even though we've got an "N" in Him, He is over the moon about us anyway, and He'll help us find the strength and courage to change. Jesus never had a problem with people who knew their shortcomings; He didn't tolerate people who faked it. Once we get real with where we actually are and our desperate need for Him, He's got a person He can do something with.

When I got home from Austin, I told Sweet Maria all about my trip and Randy's terrific church and the rental-car guy. I told her how I sat in line and filled the bucket with patience. She nodded as I waved my arms, and she looked at me with a grin and a twinkle in her eye as I told her about how much progress I had made in being patient. When I was all done, I asked her what she thought about everything I was learning. With the sincerity of Mother Teresa and the wisdom of the ages, she leaned over to me and whispered, "Get a bigger bucket."

As I think about it now, I realize I looked pretty silly walking around with my bucket, but I probably look even sillier walking around with all my pride and selfishness and impatience. Even more so to the people who were closest to me—the ones my life wasn't working for. The same is probably true for you and the ones you love. Now, when I'm feeling overwhelmed by distractions or someone hurts my feelings or I'm feeling a little impatient, I grab my bucket. I still mess up more often than I want to. When I do, instead of beating myself up, wishing I were the guy who had it all figured out, I hear the gentle and kind voice of Jesus reminding me once again to stop laying sod where He's planting seed in my life. His reason is simple: He's more interested in making us grow than having us look finished. He wants me to realize I'm just not quite there yet.

CHAPTER 18

Croc Drop

We all go to "our" church.

I received a call from a small church in Alabama, and they asked if I'd speak at a gathering they were having. The guy who called said the place they were meeting was located in a small town I hadn't heard of before. It was going to be a lot of travel to get there, so I asked him to tell me a little more about the event.

"Well," he said with a terrific Southern accent and a pause, "we're having a croc drop."

"A croc drop?" I asked in amazement.

"Yep," he said.

"I'm in!" I shot back.

What more information does a guy need? I started rearranging everything I had on the calendar and bought a plane ticket. I felt like I had turned back into a junior high school kid who was about to take the tires off the principal's car.

Growing up in Southern California, I'd never been to a croc

drop before. I hadn't even seen a crocodile except on the Discovery Channel. I was envisioning how terrific it was going to be when the crocodiles began falling like balloons from the ceiling when I walked in. Kind of like when a president gets elected. Except the balloons would have big teeth and tails and they'd look really dangerous until the people there made belts and shoes and luggage out of them. I wondered if the crocodiles bounced when they hit the ground or if they just started biting people on the fly. These are important things to know. *What does a guy wear to a croc drop anyway?* I wondered. *Camouflage? Body armor? Nothing at all?* I wasn't sure.

I arrived for the event and made my way to a huge warehouse where the croc drop was going to happen. I got to the door, puffed out my chest, took a deep breath, and said out loud, "Bring it!" as I opened the door and walked inside. It only took me a moment to realize I'd gotten something terribly wrong. This place wasn't filled with crocodiles as I'd expected; it was filled with potatoes. Lots of potatoes. Thousands of them. It seemed all potatoes ever grown were in there. And lots of people too. Not everyone in Alabama, but most of them.

A youngish guy came up to me, thrust out his hand, and introduced himself as the guy who had invited me. I was still a little confused and kept glancing up at the ceiling. I didn't want to be rude, but after a couple of awkward minutes of small talk, I drummed up the courage to ask him, "So where are the crocodiles, and where do they drop from?"

He looked at me for a second, half-grinning, and cocked his head. "Crocodiles?"

"Yeah," I said. "You know, for the croc drop."

A huge grin grew over his face and he exploded into a belly laugh. "This isn't a croc drop. It's a crop drop!"

"A crop drop?" I asked, more than a little disappointed.

That would explain all the potatoes, but I still didn't get it.

He told me there were a couple of fields just outside of town. When the crops are picked by machine, many of the potatoes are left on the ground afterward. All the churches in the area gather together and glean the fields to get the potatoes the machines missed and then bag them for the poor and hungry in the community.

"We're all just bagging potatoes here. We want to make good use of what gets passed over."

It was such a beautiful picture of what the church is and who we're supposed to be. Inside the warehouse, there were no name tags, no members, no separate identities, no building programs, no matching shirts, and no discussions about theology or who was right and who was wrong. It was just a bunch of people bagging passed-over food to give away to people in the community who probably felt passed over too. People who are becoming love lose all the labels because they know they don't need them.

The night before Jesus died, His prayer for us was that we would be "one." He knew what it was like to be "one" with His Father, and He said He wanted that for us. It was a prayer for unity, not sameness. He knew the gospel wasn't a bunch of rules to obey; it was a Person to follow and be one with. He wanted us to live into the beautiful, unique creations God made us to be. Simply put, we can be "one" without being each other.

The people in the warehouse that night didn't see themselves as a bunch of churches coming together to participate in a program. They were one church, living out its purpose. I bet if you asked them where they go to church, they'd point to everybody helping out and tell you they all go to "our" church. Our church is made of people like you and me whom Jesus didn't pass over just because we messed up. He didn't give us a membership; He gave us a message. It's the same message I saw carried that night by a bunch of people bagging potatoes in Alabama. They realized if following Jesus didn't lead them to the poor and the hungry and the isolated, then they weren't actually following Jesus.

The story is literally as old as time, but God loved what He created in the universe so much, He made people to enjoy it. Perhaps we thought because God made us, we should make something nice for Him in return, so we built Him a bunch of buildings and started going to them on Sunday mornings and Wednesday nights. I love church buildings. I spend almost every weekend in one. The problem is, God said He doesn't dwell in buildings made by men; instead, we can find Him in the people He made who want their lives to look like His. Does He use the buildings? You bet. Does He love it when we gather for worship in them? Absolutely. Nothing delights Him more. Does He need them? Not for a minute. He's got us, we've got Him, and He's given us each other. It's been His plan from the beginning. Should we meet together as a community around Jesus? Yes, constantly. Where? Everywhere. You pick. He wants our hearts; He doesn't care about the address where it happens.

I spoke to a guy once who said the church had hurt his feelings, so he was leaving it. I told him, "You can't leave the church, you *are* the church." That guy is part of our church. Your church is part of our church too. Even if you don't think you go to a church, you're part of our church. At our church there is nothing to join, just Jesus. This is probably why Jesus told His friends, where two or more people who follow Him go, He's there.

I get asked all the time, "Where do you go to church?" As you might imagine, my answer is always the same: I go to our church. I'm not trying to dodge the question when I say this; I'm trying to be accurate. I learned this at a croc drop.

There's a pastor friend of mine who doesn't really have his own church. Instead, for years he brought together people in his community from lots of different churches. He just wanted them to be one the way Jesus told His Father He wanted us to be one.

There were a couple thousand people who came together every month or two, and my friend asked me to speak at one of the gatherings. They didn't really need a name for what they were doing. They're ordinary folks, like you and me, who think it's enough just to be together, give thanks to God, and leave all the names and labels and distractions behind.

Sadly, I received a call from my friend a couple of days before I came out to speak. He told me he'd just received word that his son, who was eight at the time, had been diagnosed with leukemia. There's no good version of this disease, but his son got a bad version.

"Oh no. Shouldn't we cancel the event?" I said into the heavy phone in my hand.

He told me, "No. Honestly, I need to be around people this week more than ever."

I flew out a few days later and was blown away by the unity this group had developed over their years together. As I finished my talk, I saw my friend sitting in the front row looking at the floor. It's a tradition in some faith communities to lay hands on someone who is hurting. It wasn't part of my faith tradition, and if you haven't seen this done before, it's not a big mystical thing. It's just a way to show support and love and community. I was thinking about doing that, but honestly, it would just be the two guys next to him and three people behind touching him and the people in row fifty would just be touching the people in row forty-nine. Then I had an idea. What if we crowd-surfed him?

My friend looked a little surprised when I asked everyone to stand up. I asked four strong guys to hoist him up over their heads and told everyone instead of symbolically laying hands on him, we were going to *actually* lay hands on him while we crowd-surfed him. Before I was finished getting the sentence out, they already had my friend in the air and had passed him a few rows back. He laid back with his arms outstretched for the next half hour as thousands of hands were laid on him. He was a guy wrapped in agony and enveloped in love. This is who we are and what we were made to do as a community. That's our church.

We don't need to just talk about lifting others up in prayer when they're hurting. Actually lift one another up instead. I don't mean this as a metaphor. Seriously, walk up behind someone who is hurting and lift them right off the ground. Don't be creepy about it, but do it. You won't need to tell them you're praying for them—they'll know. If you're wondering where Jesus' friends are, just find people whose feet are a foot off the ground because someone else is lifting them up. You just found our church.

Sometimes we make church a lot more complicated than Jesus meant for it to be. When I was young, there was a rhyme that went, "Here is the church, and here is the steeple. Open the doors, and see all the people." I would weave my fingers together with the pointer fingers touching to make the steeple. With my palms open, I would wiggle all the "people" in the church. I bet you've done the same a couple of times. It was just an amusing rhyme then, but it means a lot more to me now.

What I saw when I was young was a church wide open in my palms. All the wiggling fingers pointed out toward the world. What is a huge turnoff to the world is when it sees under the steeple a lot of the fingers pointing at each other. Every time we go to church and point fingers at each other, we betray Jesus with another kiss. At "our" church, we go there to meet Him, not to critique each other.

God calls the church His bride. It's a beautiful metaphor, full of love and anticipation and commitment. Have you ever gone to a wedding where the bride walked in and a guy in row four held up a card with a "7" on it like they do in the Olympics, whispering to the person next to him, "I've seen better"?

Of course not! The bride steals the show. Every time.

Do you know what makes the bride look terrific? It's not the fancy dress or the building or the flowers or the music. Those things are great, but what makes the bride look terrific is everyone in the room knows the groom chose her to be his and she's chosen him to be hers. The two of them can't wait to spend forever together. I think this is the reason why God calls us His bride.

This picture of the church helps me understand some of the most difficult questions I've had about how God sees all of us. It's pretty easy to understand, really. God loves us and He wants to spend forever together. We're His bride. He doesn't see all our flaws; He just sees us. God doesn't hold up a scorecard as we walk by either. He sees Jesus. It's that simple. The way our church will return to the loving and accepting place the Bible talks about is by keeping our eyes on the Groom instead of one another. We can put all the scorecards away.

Perhaps if we spent a little more time looking at the Groom, we'd start seeing ourselves the way He does. To God, we look just terrific. Does our church have problems? You bet. But He continues to pick us to spread His love to the world. I'm not sure why. To be honest, I wouldn't have. But He said He picked us, and that's all I need to know to be part of the celebration. We're the bride of Christ, not because of what we look like but because of who we are trying to act like. That's our church.

CHAPTER 19

Be. Not. Afraid.

When you have all the power, you
don't need all the words.

Our family has spent a lot of time in Africa. My son-in-law, Jon, is an engineer and a hydrologist and has spent years building underground dams in Mozambique. Lindsey now goes with him there. Maria, Richard, Ashley, and Adam have all traveled to Africa as well. When I first arrived in Uganda in 2001, the country was still in the middle of a twenty-five-year civil war fueled by Joseph Kony and the Lord's Resistance Army. I knew almost no one there. I had originally gone to Uganda to help friends whose nonprofit had gotten into some trouble with one of their projects. While I was there, I began wondering if I could be helpful to this country in some small way.

I'm a pretty good lawyer, and knowing God often uses what we're good at to guide us into what we do next, I headed for the courthouse. Maybe I could find someone there who would let me know how I could help. When I got to the courthouse, there were soldiers with machine guns at all the entrances and exits. A trial was underway against some of the president's political opponents who had been charged with treason. This was a capital crime, and it added to an already tense time for the country. The last time a trial took place for treason, under the former leader Idi Amin, it resulted in fifteen deaths by firing squad. That was years earlier, but no one knew how this one would turn out.

I saw an official-looking office with more men and machine guns around it than any of the others, so I headed there, figuring someone important must be behind the doors. I inched past the soldiers, checking the safeties on their machine guns as I passed, and entered the office through a large doorway. Behind a big wooden desk was a pleasant woman who asked how she could help me. Not knowing whose office it was, I simply asked if I could see the judge.

"Do you have an appointment?"

"Not really," I said, looking down. "But I've come eighteen thousand miles to get here."

"Just a moment," she said as she rose from her desk and disappeared behind another pair of huge doors. She came back a few moments later and said, "The judge will see you now." I hid my surprise and walked past her through the doorway, trying to act confident and lawyerly. The judge was sitting behind a massive desk, writing something, and didn't look up as I entered. When he did look up, he rose and gestured with his hand toward a seat.

The proper greeting for a judge in Uganda is "my lord." Saying this takes a little getting used to at first. Where I was raised, this is reserved for the guys in the book of Psalms talking to God. In San

Diego, we're also more likely to call someone "dude" than "lord." But I had practiced in the mirror that morning until I had it, so I was ready. The judge asked why I was in Uganda and I told him I was a lawyer and the only qualifications I had were that I loved justice, I loved people, and I wanted to find a place I could help.

We talked about his kids and my kids and hope and how Ugandan courts had been closed in the northern half of the country for more than a decade while the civil war raged. As our time was wrapping up, we both stood up. I came around the desk and gave him a big hug. I think he was a little taken aback. I told him I was a hugger. He told me he wasn't, and this was actually the reason he has guys with machine guns guarding his office. I took out my key ring, slipped off the key to the front door of our house, and gave it to him. I had my first friend in Uganda.

It turned out this was no ordinary judge. This was the chief justice of Uganda's Supreme Court. That would explain the machine guns. He had written Uganda's constitution when they declared independence from Britain, and he was the second-most powerful man in the country. Sometimes we wait for permission or a plan or a calling or a mystical sign from God before we get started. It could work that way, I suppose. What I've found, though, is when we're looking for a plan, God often sends us a person.

I've been an adjunct professor at Pepperdine's law school for quite a few years. Some people find it hard to imagine me teaching at one of our country's top law schools. I know, me too. My first year there, I thought I needed to play the part and act very scholarly. You know, smoke a pipe, wear a sweater-vest, and run my fingers through my beard. That kind of stuff. Now on the first day of class, I just wave my arms over my head and tell everyone, "You're going to pass the bar exam!"

The class I teach is on failure. Each week, I bring in one of my friends who has screwed up in front of pretty much all the people on earth. Having failed big at least a couple of times is almost a requirement to be my friend—otherwise we won't have much in common. The objective of the class is simple. I don't want these young lawyers to think they're winners because they happen to win a case, or losers because they happen to lose one. I want them to know they're participants because they tried. They're just Tree #4.

I brought Jason, one of my good friends, into class. He made one of the most viral videos in the history of the Internet. He's bright and engaging and sensitive and endlessly creative. In less than a week, his video was downloaded over one hundred million times. On the morning of the eleventh day, after one hundred million people had seen the video, he invited me over to his house. We were sitting on the kitchen floor pounding waffles when something inside of him snapped and he ripped off all his clothes. I held on to him in an attempt to keep the party inside, but he got away. He ran outside and melted down on TMZ in front of millions of people. Mercifully, no one knew I was the guy holding his boxers, trying to get him back into them.

My friend had made a mistake prompted by something far beyond his control. Here's the important thing I learned from him: he doesn't think he's still naked on the corner. Many of us think of our big mistakes as disqualifying us; God sees them as preparing us. Jason is still as creative as he is courageous, and with guts and grit he sees the bright hope his future offers the world. He is dreaming, inventing, and exploring again. He's learning and giving away hope and joy again. In a word, he sees what most of us don't. He sees who he's becoming, and this is it: he's becoming love. Sometimes God uses the most difficult things in our lives to show us the most accurate things about our lives—if we have the guts to receive a little grace.

They say if you're an adjunct professor at Pepperdine, you need to have office hours, but they don't say where. I have mine on Tom Sawyer Island at Disneyland every Wednesday from ten in the morning to two in the afternoon. I tell the students at Pepperdine if they have a question and ninety-five bucks, they should come and see me. I'm willing to bet I'm the only guy at the Magic Kingdom with a laptop and a stack of papers to grade. What's kind of funny is there have only been a handful of times when I've gone to my office on Tom Sawyer Island and had fewer than ten people waiting for me.

There are plenty of places I could go to meet people, I suppose. Pepperdine's law school has a bunch of conference rooms. I've even heard there's an office I can use, but I've never gone. I meet people at Disneyland because where we meet shapes the discussions we'll have. We've all experienced this, but few of us put this idea into practice when we're setting our meetings. It's not silly to meet on a set of swings or a movie set, at a park or an airplane museum or at Build-A-Bear. I've used all of them. Each is engaging and creative and fun in its own way. Location drives content. It's why we should be as picky about where we talk as we are about what we actually discuss. If you have the right conversation at the right place, you just had the right conversation. However, if you have the right conversation at the wrong place, you just had the wrong conversation.

I don't think people grow old. I think they just lose their imaginations and end up looking old. Tom Sawyer Island reminds me of who I am and who I'm becoming. It's a place Walt Disney created where people wouldn't stand forever in lines and could run and jump and remember who they really are. Most people spend more time looking for their car keys than they do their imaginations. I want to keep my imagination close where I can find it. I find it every Wednesday at my office.

After several trips to Uganda, I asked the chief justice if he would ever consider coming to America. He said if he came to the United States someday, he'd like to see my office because I'd seen his. A few years later, when the chief justice arrived at Los Angeles International Airport, I asked him if he still wanted to see my office. He said he wanted it to be our first stop. We drove past all the high-rises towering above Wilshire Boulevard in Los Angeles and kept heading south. I'm sure he wondered more than once where we were going. A short time later, we pulled into the parking lot at Disneyland. He stepped out of the car and asked me, "You have an office here?"

"Of course I do," I shot back. "You should see my pirate ship!"

I had Mickey Mouse ears made for him in advance. Embroidered

on the front were the words *The Chief* in yellow stitching. As I
slipped on his ears, I told the chief justice it was kind of a rule that
anybody coming to Disneyland for the first time had to wear the
Mickey Mouse ears all day long. So he did.

I took him on the Jungle Cruise so he would know what Africa
really looked like, then we made our way to the Indiana Jones ride.
When the ride ended, I turned to him, my arms still up in the
air, and asked, "Wasn't that just like the movie?" The chief justice
looked puzzled and asked, "There's a movie?" I knew we'd never
run out of things to talk about. Later, he came over to our house
and pulled his key out of his pocket. He slipped it in the lock and
turned it tentatively. Of course it worked, and he turned to me
with a mile-wide grin.

Before we left Disneyland, the chief justice and I took the raft
over to Tom Sawyer Island. We sat at my office and talked again
about kids and justice and hope. Our conversation took a sober
turn when we talked about witch doctors and child sacrifice. To
modern ears, this sounds like something that might have happened
a hundred years ago or more, but it's happening now. Almost a
thousand children are abducted by witch doctors in a single year in
Uganda alone. The belief among witch doctors is that the head or
blood or private parts of their victims have magical powers. They
bury them in foundations of buildings and use them for ceremonies and for other horrible practices. Mothers will protect their
newborn baby girls by piercing their ears at birth, hoping they'll no
longer represent a perfect sacrifice.

Thousands of people in Uganda had been affected by witch
doctors, yet in the history of the country no one had ever taken

on a witch doctor in the legal system. In part, this is because the young victims never survive. The other reality is that many, including some judges, are afraid of the witch doctors. I asked the chief justice if he would let me be part of a trial against a witch doctor if we ever found a victim who lived. He said he would. It was the right conversation at the right place.

I've been traveling to Uganda regularly now for almost two decades with a nonprofit I started called Love Does, which has the goal of helping children throughout the world. We've tried cases involving minors wrongfully stuck in prisons, and we operate schools and safe houses in Uganda, Iraq, Somalia, Nepal, and India for kids who need an education and for young girls who have been rescued from horrible circumstances.

On a trip to a prison in the bush in Uganda, far from any major city, I met a young girl. She was thirteen years old and had been in prison for two years. I asked the warden what the charge was and he said she was being held for kidnapping. She had been accused of the crime, taken to prison the same day, and remained locked up for two years without ever stepping into a courtroom.

It's impossible to completely read someone in a short visit, but I just wasn't getting the "I'm a kidnapper" vibe from the girl, so I asked her what had happened. She told me she had been asked to take a baby girl to the child's mother in a neighboring village. You and I would have asked more questions, of course, but she was a young peasant girl who was used to doing what she was told. She took the baby to a hut and put the child in the arms of someone she thought was the baby's mother. As soon as she stepped outside the hut, she heard the baby crying. It wasn't the normal cry of an infant. It was a desperate scream.

It turned out this wasn't the baby's mother at all. She had been tricked into taking the baby to a witch doctor for a child sacrifice. Before the baby's life was taken, the peasant girl rushed back in, grabbed the child, and ran back home. By then, the villagers had realized the baby was missing, and when she returned with the child, she was arrested.

The warden was present during this conversation, so I asked him which jail held the witch doctor who was going to sacrifice the child. I wanted to get the other side of the story. The warden shook his head; no arrest had been made. No questions had been asked. No one went after the witch doctor. "What?" I almost yelled. It was the moment I decided I was going to do something.

Someone once asked me what I would write if I only had six words for my autobiography. Here's what I came up with: *What if we weren't afraid anymore?* Throughout history, God has spoken three words more often than any others when the people He loved were scared and confused, lost or lonely, paralyzed or stuck. In those times, He usually didn't make a big speech. He just said to His people, *Be. Not. Afraid.*

The police don't arrest witch doctors because they're afraid of them, and the judges don't try cases against witch doctors for the same reason. As I drove away from the prison after meeting that thirteen-year-old girl, two things happened. First, I got hold of a judge and we set a date to bring her case to trial, which later resulted in her release and return to her family. The second thing was equally subtle and powerful. It wasn't an audible voice, but it was as if three words were tattooed on my heart that day. I bet you know what they were. I knew we were going to find a witch doctor and bring them to justice. I wanted every witch doctor to know we weren't afraid of them anymore.

CHAPTER 20

Witch Doctors and
Witness Stands

Courage comes in all sizes.

Kabi was head of all the witch doctors in his region of Northern Uganda. He was my age and had no hair on his head, no stubble on his face, and no smile. It was like all the hate in his life had congregated on his face. It was worn and stern, and his blood-shot eyes had a yellowish hue. Kabi was the most evil person I've ever met.

An eight-year-old boy, who we'll call Charlie, was walking home from school when Kabi abducted him. Kabi took Charlie into the bush, cut off his private parts, and left him for dead. But Charlie didn't die. Kabi was arrested a short time later, and for the first time in Uganda's history, we had one of the leaders of the witch doctors and a victim who was alive.

Once I learned about Charlie, I immediately got on a plane to go see my friend "The Chief." Because we'd had the right conversation at the right place on Tom Sawyer Island, I felt a huge sense of anticipation that something big was unfolding. The plane couldn't fly fast enough.

When I landed in Uganda, I drove several hours into the bush to meet Charlie for the first time. Charlie was dressed in loose clothing and looked down, afraid to make eye contact. He had been through much and it showed. Earlier that day, Charlie had identified his attacker in a lineup from a distance at the prison. I asked him a few questions, but it was clear he was in no condition to talk. Our conversations would come much later.

After this first encounter with Charlie, I went to meet with a high court justice to ask if he would be willing to have the case against Kabi brought to trial in his court. His office felt heavy as we spoke, as if it were weighed down by the tremendous gravity of the moment. We both knew what we were discussing. This would be Uganda's first case in which the death penalty was being sought against a witch doctor. It was uncharted territory. It might work, and it might be a total failure. What then?

The witch doctors had gripped the whole country with fear.

When we set out to bring the case against Kabi to trial, I have to admit I was more than a little skeptical about whether we'd be able to find a judge brave enough to take on this case. All the odds said we'd strike out, but within a week this courageous judge agreed. We had a courtroom and a trial date for Uganda's first case against a witch doctor. It turned out we weren't the only ones who wanted a fight.

When the local witch doctors found out the judge had taken

the case, they began appearing at his home and did some pretty creepy things. He could have backed out. Many would have. Instead, he surrounded his home with guards who had plenty of guns. Great love often involves tremendous risk. This amazing judge was willing to push back against the darkness. He was turning into love.

The date of the trial was set several months out. Prior to the trial, I made several trips back and forth to Uganda to meet with the witnesses, the police, the investigators, and Charlie. The day finally came for the trial to begin. Kabi arrived in chains, surrounded by a dozen well-armed soldiers.

A few of us were staying across the street from the courthouse in a thatched hut. Our country director, who we called "Two Bunk John," had arranged everything. We brought in a projector, a generator, and a screen to give visual evidence of what happened. We had binders full of notes and legal documents to explain what the laws of the country were. One high court justice and several tribal leaders would be present. Uganda still uses the British system in the judiciary, so everyone wears white powdered wigs, black capes, and ruffled white shirts. It's impressive—even more so in this setting in the bush in Uganda. The soldiers surrounded the courthouse as the judge gaveled the room to order.

We had received permission from the judge to videotape the trial because it was a first in the country, so I purchased a new video camera that cost me more than my first two cars in college. Two Bunk John was operating the camera. At one point, I was asking questions in the trial and saw Kabi look up at John and stare at the camera. John's face turned to ash and he pulled his eye away from the eyepiece suddenly. At one of the breaks, Two Bunk showed me the video clip. As Kabi raised his head and started staring at the camera, the video fuzzed out to black-and-white static like a television that stopped working. I assumed the witch doctor's death stare was covered by Nikon's warranty, so we shared a nervous laugh, got out another camera, and got back to work. People like John who are turning into love get distracted but don't stay that way for long.

The next session in the trial would be Charlie's testimony. When the judge reconvened the trial, Charlie entered the room. He was told to tell the truth and was asked about what happened. This eight-year-old kid stood up the size of a mountain, pointed at Kabi, and said, "That's the man who tried to kill me." Charlie reminded me of another boy with five smooth stones facing a giant. That boy didn't back down, and Charlie didn't either. The courtroom was silent as everyone witnessed his courage. Without flinching, Charlie gave the details of what had happened to him.

Sometimes I've wondered what difference one person can make in the world. I have a red plate at home that says I am "very special." We get it out on birthdays. The plate doesn't make me special, though. It's the people surrounding me and my plate who make me special. The same is true for you. Still, I feel pretty small most of the time. When I saw Charlie's courage, he didn't need a plate, and he wasn't small. He cast a shadow of courage bigger than any NFL linebacker.

What is it you don't think you can do? What do you think is too big for you, or too scary, or too risky? Sometimes God whispers it and sometimes He shouts it. Whatever the volume, I bet He's always using the same three words with us:

Be. Not. Afraid.

When Charlie finished giving his testimony and had answered all the questions and cross-examinations, he got off the stand. He looked exhausted but unshaken. This was the first time since the attack he had been this close to Kabi.

I took him outside and told him how proud of him I was. I touched him on the nose and said to him, "Charlie, you were brave, you were courageous, and you weren't afraid." A small smile spread across his face.

The trial took the rest of the week to finish. A short time later, we received the judge's guilty verdict. In Uganda, once the judge signs the verdict, the custom is to take the pen, break it, and throw it off the table. Then the judge says with an unmatched finality, "What's been done today will never be undone." When the judge signed Kabi's order and said the words, it meant Kabi would never be seen again.

The word of Kabi's conviction went out to forty-one million people.

The courage of a four-foot-tall boy had changed the history of an entire nation.

We had done it—the very first witch doctor conviction in Ugandan history. I'll be honest, while sad about Charlie's loss, I was pleased with the outcome of the trial. Justice had been served, and it paved the way for a more courageous stance for these types of crimes against children.

But then something happened I didn't expect. I started wondering about Kabi.

Every fiber of my being wanted him to rot in the jail that would be his home for the rest of his life. I was okay with that. But my heart felt dark when I thought about Kabi. It felt far from God, and I didn't like it.

Jesus was talking to His friends one day and explained how He wanted us to live our lives. He pulled His friends in close and said something I bet surprised them. He didn't say they needed to use bigger words in their prayers, or go to church more, or not chew tobacco or dance. It wasn't behaviors He talked about. He said if we wanted to please God, we needed to love our enemies.

I've already told you how I've found it's a lot easier to agree with Jesus than to do what He says. The command to love our enemies is a good example. The truth is, I don't want to love mine. My enemies are creepy. They're mean and uncaring. They're selfish and full of pride. Some try to hurt little kids.

Jesus didn't come to make us look like we've got it together. He came to let us know how to be like Him. I'm all for that, but does loving my enemies include guys like Kabi? I don't think so.

But here is where I'm stopped dead in my tracks. On the day Jesus died on the cross, He was broken for us—not unlike the judge's pen. It was like God was saying, "What's been done today will never be undone."

Paul was one of the people who talked about Jesus. He

explained grace in this way: He said neither death nor life, neither angels nor demons, neither present nor future, nor any powers, neither height nor depth, nor anything else in all creation could ever separate us from the love of God.

What he was saying is the horrible things we've done won't separate us from God. They won't separate you and they won't separate me and they won't separate Kabi either. Honestly, it's hard for me to believe this. It may be hard for you too.

Jesus explained the reason He wanted us to love our enemies was so we could be *perfect*, the way His Father in heaven is perfect. Perfect? Ha! Most of us have spent our whole lives just trying to be nice some of the time, not cutting in line and only calling people names under our breath. Sure, we could give someone a small break by saying something generous after they have been awful to us. Maybe we could even forgive someone, at least on the surface, for a deep hurt they caused. Doing things like these have been the high-water mark we only hit once in a while, if at all.

Our problem following Jesus is we're trying to be a better version of us, rather than a more accurate reflection of Him. I've met very few people who didn't like Jesus. I mean, who wouldn't? It's easy to admire Jesus and think He's a nice guy. But there's a big difference between *liking* Jesus and being *like* Him, and He said we would never be able to be like Him unless we loved our enemies.

I've never wondered if someone could be perfect. I don't mean someone like Jesus, of course, but someone like you and me. I've never even heard of anyone jumping out of bed in the morning and saying their goal for the day was to be *perfect*. When I met Sweet Maria I remember thinking she was perfect, but I knew she really wasn't. I had a job once I thought was perfect for me and it was a great job, but honestly, it wasn't perfect. We don't think perfect is possible, so we just nod and agree rather than do the heavy lifting Jesus talked about to get there.

The idea that we could be *perfect* like our Father in heaven sounds like a beautiful idea but not something we could ever really achieve. I wonder if God thought loving our enemies would be just as hard. Perhaps instead of an impossible task in our lives, it's the report card on our faith. Maybe God made loving Him and our enemies the easiest way to tell whether we just agree with Jesus or if we want to be perfect like Him.

No doubt, Kabi was my enemy. But he was also my chance to become more like Jesus. And now I had a courageous teacher who was only four feet tall to guide me.

CHAPTER 21

Randy's Skill

God restores what He creates.

On the other side of the world, a man walked into the emergency room of a hospital in Los Angeles. He had been involved in a horrible accident in his woodshop. His right hand had been completely severed, and he was carrying it in his left hand. Calls were immediately made to get one of the few surgeons who would be able to deal with such a massive and complex injury. It would be hero's work, even for the world's best surgeons.

Randy arrived, scrubbed in, and began what would be an eighteen-hour surgery. With scores of labeled hemostats, he identified and numbered each of the hundreds of tendons, veins, arteries, and muscles on both sides of the injury. One by one, he reconnected them. Never flinching. Never losing concentration. He did the painstaking, nearly impossible work of reconnecting this man's hand to his body again. I saw a video of Randy a few months later shaking hands with this carpenter who had regained full use of his hand. Only a handful of the best surgeons in the world could have done this operation. Randy was one of them.

Randy loves airplanes. There aren't many he hasn't flown. He was learning how to fly a DeHavilland Beaver seaplane near Seattle. The person teaching him took him in the off-season over the border to Canada, far up an inlet. Unbeknownst to me, they landed at my lodge and walked around a little. While they were exploring, the instructor, who is a friend of mine, told Randy about a little boy in Uganda who had suffered a massive injury with a machete. He learned about a witch doctor who had committed a crime, a guilty verdict, and a little boy who was horribly disfigured.

The extent of Charlie's injuries is tough for most to imagine. Justice had been done to Kabi, but Charlie wasn't whole. Not by a far reach. There would be many challenges ahead for him. Charlie would never be able to be a father when he grew up because of the body parts he lost. At some point, Charlie's friends would no doubt find out about his disfigurement and tease him as well. He would have extensive mental and emotional healing to do in addition to the physical.

At home in San Diego, the telephone rang and I answered. The voice on the other side said, "Bob, you don't know me, but my name is Randy. I heard what happened to the kid in Uganda. I want you to know something . . ." There was a pause as I leaned into the phone. I could feel Randy's seriousness.

"I can fix him," he said.

His words hung in the airwaves.

I was polite with this stranger over the telephone but was thinking, *Buddy, you don't understand about all the things that were cut off. You can't fix that.* Sensing this, Randy continued, "I'm a surgeon at Cedars-Sinai Medical Center in Los Angeles. Really, I can fix him."

I drove to Los Angeles, and we met at a restaurant with my friend Don. Randy started drawing on a napkin what he was going to do to replace the numerous body parts Charlie had lost. Even on a napkin, it was way too much information. If they find that napkin the next time I'm going through security at the airport, I'll go to jail.

Randy explained how he would take parts from Charlie's leg and from his arm and make some new parts, but there was a caveat. Randy explained how even the best surgeons can only do so much. After the surgery, while Charlie wouldn't run the risk of being teased because some of what he lost could be replaced, he would still lack what was necessary to be able to be a biological father in the future. The kind of restoration needed for those missing body parts was simply beyond anyone's medical capability.

I hesitated after seeing how involved the surgery would be but finally had to ask, "Randy, what would the operation cost?" I was guessing millions. Without skipping a beat, Randy looked up and said, "I'll do it for nothing."

I can afford nothing, I thought. But there had to be a catch, right? While Randy might waive his fee, what about the nurses and equipment and all that stuff? It turned out there's a fantastic organization that helps cover the costs of these kinds of operations. Knowing I wouldn't be hit unexpectedly with a crazy bill, I got another plane ticket and headed back to Uganda to find Charlie in the bush in Northern Uganda.

Once I had him, he packed a few things, and we got in the car. Our first stop was the courthouse in the capital. A short time later, we stood before a Ugandan high court judge and I became Charlie's legal guardian. Charlie's father had long since abandoned him and was nowhere to be found. His mother, a peasant woman, had distanced herself from Charlie as well. I'm not judging them in this; it's just a fact and not uncommon, unfortunately.

When we got to the airport, Charlie stared out the terminal window without saying a thing. He'd never even seen an airplane before. I tried to explain the whole idea of going into the air and how safe it was, but he wasn't buying it. After a little coaxing and a couple of candy bars, we got on the plane and flew to London. When we arrived, we were holding hands as we got off the plane. Charlie asked, "Father, can we just walk the rest of the way?" I can imagine how he must have felt. I broke the bad news to him about the Atlantic Ocean and polar cap we were about to fly over. I tried not to freak him out, but I think I did again.

Once inside the terminal, I opened my laptop to see if I had any urgent messages. In my inbox was an email that stood out. The title was simple: it just said "White House" in the subject line. I have many friends who like to play pranks on me, so I immediately went down the list of suspects in my mind. It was a long list. The body of the message was brief. It read, "We'd like to meet Charlie." After a couple of quick calls, I confirmed that, incredibly, the invitation was legit. We got back on the plane with our friend, Darla, and flew to Washington, DC, where Sweet Maria met us. This kid was standing in the bush in Northern Uganda two days before and was now standing in President Obama's Oval Office.

Charlie walked over to the wall and pointed to a document hanging in a frame. "What's this?" he asked. We spent the next ten minutes talking about the Emancipation Proclamation, signed by Abraham Lincoln. Before we left, Charlie grabbed an apple from the bowl on the coffee table between two sofas and took a bite. You know, the one next to the eagle emblem in the carpet. I leaned over to Charlie and whispered, "Don't drip."

Why does God do things like this? The honest answer is, I'm not really sure, but I've got a good guess. I think He wants to blow our minds. There's a letter in the Bible Paul sent to some of his friends. He was trying to explain something similar. He acknowledged not many of the people he was writing to were wise or powerful or born into famous families. But he said God uses unbelievable things, just like what happened to Charlie, so we wouldn't keep making everything about ourselves but instead would see how powerful God is.

The next day we left Washington, DC, and flew to Los Angeles for Charlie's operation. Any kid who is headed to that kind of operation needs to go to the happiest place on earth, so I took him to Disneyland. I know several of the characters there and they made him feel special. Tinker Bell is a friend of mine and is about Charlie's size. We arranged for them to spend some time together. He kept looking at her wings and touching them in amazement. She wrapped her arms around him and told him what a brave young man he was. I think I saw the two of them lift off the ground a little as she did.

The next morning, I put Charlie in his hospital gown and got him on the gurney to be taken to the operating room. Before they rolled him into surgery, I prayed for him and Randy, then I gave Charlie a kiss on the forehead and said the words God has been saying over each of us since the beginning of time and the beginning of our lives. I whispered in his ear, "Charlie, be not afraid." By the end of the eight-hour surgery, Randy had done what he does better than anyone else in the world. Charlie was restored.

CHAPTER 22

Kabi

What we punish, God can forgive.

The minute he attacked Charlie, Kabi became my enemy. He wasn't a little evil; he was pure evil. It's easy to talk a good game about loving your enemies until you have one. I realized if I wanted big things to happen in my life, I'd need to take bigger steps and risk more than I had before, so I decided to visit Kabi in prison.

Kabi had been sent to Luzira Maximum Security Prison. Luzira is one of the scariest places on the planet. It was built in 1920 for two hundred death row inmates. There are over three thousand men in Luzira today. There are no windows in most places. If you go to Luzira, you go to die.

I contacted the warden at the Luzira prison. I gave him my name and said I'd like to see Kabi. He told me absolutely not. It was a maximum-security prison and no one gets in to see people like Kabi. I told the warden I was the honorary consul for the Republic of Uganda, and after a short pause he said, "You're in."

Kabi entered the dark room where I was waiting. He had no shoes and was wearing a torn and dirty prison uniform. When he entered, he took a knee and told me how bad he felt about what he had done to Charlie. Skeptical, I thought he was just sorry because we had caught and punished him. He told me what it was like growing up the son of a witch doctor and what witchcraft had done to him over the course of his life. Then he said something that stunned me. He said, "I know I'm going to die in here. What I really need is forgiveness."

His words hung in the air.

Forgiveness?

For a witch doctor who tried to sacrifice Charlie?

My immediate reaction was—absolutely not. He'd tried to kill the little boy I love. But something inside of me had started to change. The change hadn't been nearly fast enough, but it was nevertheless happening. I didn't see a killer in front of me; I felt like I was looking at a criminal hanging on a cross next to Jesus. I thought of the words Jesus spoke to that criminal: "Today you will be with me in paradise." There wasn't a quiz Jesus gave to the criminal to get in. He didn't ask the guy about his positions on a host of social issues. He didn't ask him to change his behaviors or say a prayer first. He just said, "You're in." Standing in a dark room next to death row is a long way from paradise.

Kabi and I talked for a while about his family and what was important to him. I talked about my family and what was most important to me. We talked about what I was learning but still didn't have figured out yet about love and grace and forgiveness and Jesus. Then something happened that will forever shape my understanding about the things Jesus talked about. Kabi said he wanted to put his faith and life in the strong and kind arms of Jesus.

When he did this, you could say he was "coming to Christ," as people in many faith communities would. But in a way, I was, too, because I was moving away from just agreeing with Jesus to doing what He said when He talked about loving my enemy. What Kabi and I are both learning about love and grace and forgiveness is that none of us needs to fully understand it to fully receive it.

I've met with Kabi quite a few times since he began his adventure with Jesus inside the walls of Luzira. When I do see him, I don't see a felon anymore. I see a guy trying to follow Jesus just like I am. While our life experiences and circumstances could not be more different, it turns out many of the problems we have turning into the men we want to be are the same.

After one of my meetings with Kabi outside of his cell, I asked the warden if anyone had come to talk to the inmates about what Jesus said our lives could look like with Him at the center. At first he waved me off, but then, as if I'd done a Jedi move, he said he'd let Kabi talk to them.

A couple of trips later, Kabi and I stood, holding hands, in the courtyard of Luzira Maximum Security Prison with my son

Richard and a few other friends. I listened while Kabi told three thousand dying men about the new life he had started with Jesus. I know what many of them were thinking:

Wait, this is Kabi the witch doctor. The evil guy.

Jesus?

Him?

Unbelievable!

Kabi spoke for thirty minutes. Honestly, I've never heard anyone hack the gospel message worse than Kabi did that day. His message was garbled and halting, and he barely got anything right. By the time he was done, I wondered if I even believed in Jesus anymore. But here's the thing: every guy in that place knew who Kabi was and what he had done, and more than a few knew I was the guy who put him there. Our standing in the courtyard together, not as enemies but as brothers, filled in all the words Kabi had messed up about Jesus. This is the story Jesus came to tell in your life, my life, and Kabi's life. He said He would turn us into love if we were willing to leave behind who we used to be.

When Kabi finished giving the best-worst sermon I've ever heard, hundreds of guys started walking toward us. Kabi picked up a water bottle, as did a couple of our other friends, and he started baptizing the other prisoners. At first, I was thinking, *Wait, you can't do that, Kabi! You hardly know anything about your faith, you know almost none of the doctrine, and you're a killer too.* But while I rattled through all the reasons he couldn't, Kabi kept splashing water over the heads of these men, inviting them to begin the adventure of becoming love themselves. I realized in that moment Kabi probably knows more about Jesus and forgiveness than most of us.

Was this how it was supposed to happen? Yes and no, I suppose. Kabi had been responsible for unthinkable pain in other people's lives and had experienced tremendous loss in his own. He's not a guy who's comfortable like me. He's a guy who is desperate enough for Jesus that he's willing to make huge changes in his life. Does he have the knowledge? Nope. Jesus chose fishermen who rarely got their nets on the right side of the boat. By all accounts, even after they had been with Jesus for three years, they still didn't fully understand who He was. They were imperfect, flawed, and had failed—sometimes big. I was reminded again how grace never seems fair until you need some.

It's hard to ignore that most of the people doing the talking from up front are guys like me who seem pretty nice and are relatable. They make us feel comfortable. Yet the people Jesus used more often were the ones who had messed up big and were desperate like Kabi.

When Kabi was done baptizing the death row inmates, he turned and walked deliberately toward me. When he reached me, he grabbed my hands. He looked me in the eyes and said in a strong and kind voice, "Bob, I forgive you."

"Wait, what?" This took me by surprise.

Hold on, you're the bad guy! You can't forgive me, I was thinking. *You're the guy who is a convict. You're the guy who was wrong, who failed, who hurt people, who caused tremendous pain. You don't know anything close to what I know about Jesus. I just heard you say a bunch of stuff about Jesus that wasn't even right.*

But then I realized what was happening. We had just been reading together what Jesus said to His friends about loving our enemies. Kabi knew if I was *his* enemy, he couldn't be *perfect* like his Father in heaven was, and that's what he wanted bad enough to do something about it.

In that moment, standing in the prison courtyard, I didn't see a witch doctor I helped convict. I saw Jesus, standing barefoot in Kabi's clothes. I saw a guy who was becoming love.

CHAPTER 23

Where Do You Want to Go?

Big love takes us to high places.

Every one of my kids went on a ten-year-old birthday adventure with Dad. For each of them, it always started with the question, "Where do you want to go?" This question wasn't intended to ask, *What do you want to see?* It was more important than that, more charged with possibility. "Where do you want to go?" really meant, "Who are you becoming, and where can we go to help you get closer to that?" Lindsey, our oldest, chose London for high tea because she's half Mary Poppins and all courage. Richard chose climbing Half Dome because he never backs down from a good challenge. Adam chose to ride across the desert on dirt bikes because, even then, he was a guy who loved adventure.

Guess who turned ten? Charlie!

I felt like I was ten years old all over again when I got on my knees and asked him in my most enthusiastic voice, "Charlie, where do you want to go?"

He didn't miss a beat and shouted, "Mount Kilimanjaro!"

I wasn't expecting that one at all. I asked him if he would rather go back to Disneyland or to Sea World, or maybe we could go to one of those indoor climbing gyms? Not a chance. His mind was made up. He wanted to climb the highest mountain in Africa. I think it's because he wanted to prove to himself he could ascend just about anything. A few months later, I got mountaineering clothes and two plane tickets, and we headed for Tanzania.

When we got to the foot of Mount Kilimanjaro, someone pointed up toward the cloud-covered mountaintop and asked, "Doesn't that look awesome?" I looked at him and just shook my head. I wanted to hurl. The mountain is 19,341 feet tall, and we were at the bottom of it. Actually, I was standing in a ditch at the time, so that made it three feet taller. I asked around to find out how the mountain got its name. I figured there was a reason it had the word *kill* in it. Because it's the tallest mountain in Africa and covered in snow at the top, it turns out people sometimes die trying to climb it.

Charlie, a couple of friends, and I started hiking up the mountain behind our guide. People have asked me what the views were like going up Kilimanjaro. I've told them I don't know. The whole way up, I just kept my eyes fixed on the guide's boots and never looked up. A few times he went over a rock when I would have rather gone around it. But if he went over it, I went over it. Other times he went around a rock I would have rather gone over. But if he went around it, I went around it too. Here's what I learned: when you've got a guide you can trust, you don't have to worry about the path you're on. It's the same lesson I've been learning about Jesus. I'm just trying to follow love's lead.

We walked for forty miles to the top of the mountain and down again, and the guide never tripped once. By contrast, it seemed I tripped every three or four steps. But do you know what happened every time I tripped? I just bumped into the guide again. Even though it happened often, the guide never turned around and gave me the hairy eyeball or told me to get my balance. He just knew I was following him closely. I think Jesus feels the same way about us. We're all going to trip as we try to follow Him through the difficult terrain of our lives. But when we do, we'll bump into Him all over again. Following Jesus means climbing, tripping, dusting ourselves off, and climbing some more. Faith isn't a business trip walked on a sidewalk; it's an adventure worked out on a steep and sometimes difficult trail.

I was in a big hurry when we started climbing Kilimanjaro. It was a mixture of fear and excitement and the buzz from downing a half-dozen Hershey bars. I was also looking for a bathroom. The guide shook his head at me as I hopped off rocks and jumped over logs. Every few minutes, he would say to me, "Bob. Pole, pole." I asked what this meant. In Swahili, "pole, pole" means "slowly, slowly."

I can't lie; for a guy who does everything fast, that's hard advice to receive and even harder advice to follow. By the end of the first day, though, as I laid down in my tent, sore, beat up, and with every muscle on fire, I knew why he'd been saying, "Pole, pole." It's hard to walk with Jesus and run ahead of Him at the same time. Yet I've been doing that my whole life. I've misunderstood going slow as lacking enthusiasm and going fast as joy. I've confused patience as a lack of will and activity as purpose.

What I learned from our guide is I could either run fast or get to the top of the mountain. I couldn't do both. We need to decide the same in our faith. It's easy to confuse busyness with progress and accomplishments with pleasing Jesus. Every day we get to decide whether we're really following Jesus or treating Him like He's just a Sherpa carrying our stuff.

It took five days, but I made it to the top of Kilimanjaro. My first thought at the summit was *Where's the air?* as I grabbed my throat. Brave little Charlie made it to 16,400 feet. This was to be his personal summit. To give context, this was higher than the summit of Mount Rainier in North America. That's not bad for a four-foot-tall kid who had just come through a big operation. Before Charlie headed back down the mountain with one of the guides, we had a ceremony. I had brought fifteen medals with me and started pinning them on Charlie's jacket. I said, "Charlie, you're brave," and pinned on the first medal. I said, "Charlie, you're courageous," and pinned on the second one. Medal after medal hung on his chest as I spoke words of truth and encouragement and love over him. As I put the last medal on him, I said, "Charlie, you're a mountain climber!" and gave him a hug. He looked like Colin Powell when he walked off that mountain.

The most important part of our ceremony wasn't what I said or all the medals. It was what I *didn't* say. You see, I didn't tell Charlie how far he had to go. I said, "Charlie, look how far you've come." People who are becoming love celebrate how far the people around them have come. They're constantly asking the question, "Where do you want to go?" Then they help the people around them get there.

Go do that with the people you love, including your enemies. Don't talk to them about their failures and the dark places they've been. Talk to them about who they're becoming and the bright hope that is their future. Speak truthful and wise words over them. Bring a few medals too. As you put the last one on their chest, look them in the eye and tell them, "Look how far you've come." Knowing that the journey you and I are on never really ends, we can ask the people we love one of the most important questions ever conceived.

"Where do you want to go?"

CHAPTER 24

Graduation Day

Love always multiplies itself.

Ever since the trial against Kabi, I've been meeting with witch doctors. My daughter-in-law, Ashley, who is also an attorney, got in a car with a friend and traveled around the country educating Ugandan high court judges on what the law is and how to bring these cases to trial. When I go to Uganda now, I send out word on the bush radio in the North that the honorary consul of Uganda has arrived and all the witch doctors are required to meet with me at the king's hut. They aren't, of course, but I'm a lawyer and I make them believe they are. The crazy part is this: they come. Hundreds and hundreds of them. I've met with almost a thousand witch doctors so far. Some of them are pretty creepy. Several have brought little dolls that look like me, and they stick pins in them while I talk. It's a little like being a pastor at some churches, I suppose. But we're not afraid of these guys. They've got nothing compared to the kind of power love has.

Before I meet with witch doctors in the king's hut, I'll go out into the bush and set up a sting. I have a camera that looks like a watch and another that looks like a pen. I go to a village, posing as a wealthy businessman from Kampala, and I ask the local witch doctor if he would help me find a kid for a child sacrifice if I needed one. Sadly, without exception, they offer to find one for thirty dollars.

Later, when I meet with all the witch doctors in the king's hut, I show them the video from the sting, and I tell them, "You see this guy? He's as good as dead. You even talk about sacrificing a kid, it's over for you too." I try to absolutely terrify them. By the looks of their big eyes and body language, it usually works.

Because I'm learning about loving my enemies, I don't stop there. People who are becoming love don't just use tough talk; they do difficult things. So after I scare the wits out of the witch doctors, I get on my knees and I wash their feet. When I do, I don't know who's more freaked out—them or me. I'm guessing me, because I'm not a toe guy. Here's the thing: loving people the way Jesus did either changes everything in us or it changes nothing. It can't just change a couple of things. But, it can change a couple of things at a time. If you want to become love, what will it change for you?

We're all learning about loving our enemies. Draw a circle around yourself and go love the people in that circle. Fill it with difficult people, the ones you've been avoiding, the ones you disagree with, the ones who are hard to get along with. Go find a couple of witch doctors.

I bring my friends with me now when I meet with witch doctors. Honestly, it's blowing our minds. Gregg has been a friend of mine for years, and we've traveled together to Uganda dozens of times. After he washed the feet of one of the witch doctors, the witch doctor kneeled and asked Gregg if he could now wash *his* feet. I watched this go down from across the room. It was a beautiful, tear-filled moment for us all. The witch doctor was just as blown away at what was happening as Gregg was. I think this is exactly the kind of stuff Jesus talked about when He said we needed to love our enemies. Jesus said being right with Him meant loving people who got things wrong.

On one trip, before we left, I asked the new leader of the witch doctors what they needed. I was surprised by the answer. He said, "People think we have power, so they want us around, but they don't really like us, so we're very isolated." I told him I was a lawyer and knew exactly how he felt.

"But most of us don't even know how to read or write," he continued.

Loving your enemies doesn't just mean learning about them or being nice to them or tolerating them. It means helping them.

So I started a witch doctor school.

I know, I know, I know. Don't freak out. Sometimes I wonder if this is crazy, but then I see what has been happening in the witch doctors' lives and I don't think so anymore. We don't teach them how to be witch doctors. They already know how to do that. We teach the witch doctors at our school how to read and write. We have hundreds of witch doctors currently enrolled in the school and have graduated hundreds more. Get this: the only books we have in the witch doctor school to teach them how to read are the Bible and *Love Does*. If you've read either of these, you've been reading their textbooks.

Bad guys who used to sacrifice children are now learning their ABCs, and do you know what? Things are changing, and not just for the witch doctors. One of the biggest changes has been in my own heart—I'm learning to love these people who used to be my enemies. I'm moving beyond just agreeing with Jesus to actually doing what He said to do. Truth be known, my life is probably changing as much as theirs.

I've seen changes in the lives of the witch doctors as they experience the kind of love and acceptance Jesus talked about. Our Ugandan friends who are afraid of witch doctors think we're nuts. We do too. Loving people the way Jesus did means being constantly misunderstood. People who are becoming love don't care. They will do whatever it takes to reach whoever is hurting.

We recently graduated our third class from the witch doctor school. Most of these witch doctors have more joy than teeth. Incredibly, we got the government to recognize their accomplishments. They now receive certificates of literacy issued from the Republic of Uganda at their graduation. Who could have imagined this would be possible? The answer is simple: Jesus did. Loving our enemies has always been His idea, not ours. The people who creep us out aren't obstacles to having faith; they're opportunities to understand it.

Our graduation ceremonies are unlike anything you could imagine. There's no public display of affection in Uganda. Nevertheless, as I give the witch doctors their diplomas, I hold their faces between my hands and kiss them on the forehead. (I want to be every witch doctor's first kiss.) I look into some pretty creepy sets of eyes and tell them who they're becoming and how far they've come as leaders in their villages and communities. Then, as I pin a medal on their graduation gown, I whisper to each witch doctor, just loud enough for them to hear, "Don't. Make me. Kill you." They're not sure whether I'm joking or not. I'm okay with that tension. We can speak truth to power.

I remind them of the consequences for any witch doctor involved in human sacrifice. I let them know there will be a trial, and after they're convicted, they'll never be seen again. There is no love without justice, but there is no justice without love. I don't think we have any business telling people what to change in their lives unless we're willing to change a couple of things in ours. For me, this means taking a step back from my pride, washing feet, and treating my enemies with the kind of selfless love Jesus didn't just talk about but demonstrated.

Not long ago, I got a call at midnight. I was out cold when the phone rang. The call was from two witch doctors from the witch doctor school.

They said, "A little boy has been abducted by a new witch doctor in town. He's taken the child into the bush for a child sacrifice, but we know where he is." There was a pause. Then the two witch doctors asked, "Should we go get the child?"

By this time, I was standing on top of the bed in my boxers, shouting, "Get the kid!"

Four hours later, I received a short text message from these two witch doctors who used to do unthinkable wrongs but have now experienced the power of love and acceptance and grace at our school. Here's the message I received:

"We've rescued the child."

"He's with his mother."

And a moment later, I received a text message that simply read: "Love does."

I lost it.

Maybe you thought you were simply coming to the end of a book. What if I told you this was actually an intervention and all the people you know have been calling and asking me to break some news to you: You can no longer continue to be the person you've been? What are you going to let go of? Who is it you don't get? Who don't you understand? Who have you been playing it safe with, while politely keeping your distance? Who has been mean or rude or flat wrong or creeps you out? Don't tell them all your opinions; give them all your love. I know it's hard for you. It's hard for me too. But I'm learning I have to follow Jesus' example and follow His lead if I'm going to follow in His steps. Even when we feel like we can't muster the strength and humility to love our enemies, the truth is we can.

If you do this, I can promise two things will happen. First, it will be messy. Sometimes *ugly* messy. You'll also be misunderstood— you might not even understand yourself anymore. The second thing is just as true: you'll grow. And people who are growing fall forward and bump into Jesus all over again.

Obeying Jesus when it comes to loving difficult people is hard. I'm still working on it. I'm sure it will take the rest of my life. The heavy lifting is worth it, though. Difficulties and setbacks will give us the chance to go back or lean forward once again. I'm convinced heaven is watching us, knowing full well all that will be left standing in the end is our love. I bet our spouses, kids, and friends are watching too.

If you want to become love, stop just agreeing with Jesus. Go call someone right now. Lift them up in ways they can't lift themselves. Send them a text message and say you're sorry. I know they don't deserve it. You didn't either. Don't put a toe in the water with your love; grab your knees and do a cannonball. Move from the bleachers to the field and you won't ever be the same.

Don't just love the people who are easy to love; go love the difficult ones. If you do this, Jesus said you'd move forward on your journey toward being more like Him. Equally important, as you practice loving everybody, always, what will happen along the way is you'll no longer be who you used to be. God will turn you into love.

EPILOGUE

It's been a busy year. I got malaria on a trip to Uganda and almost died. I could have avoided it by taking a nickel pill and drinking a half glass of water. You can probably avoid some of what's been killing your joy just as easily.

The Lodge that took us twenty-two years to build burned to the ground, along with everything we loved inside of it. We keep reminding each other we're sad but not stuck. Memories aren't flammable.

Carol is still in heaven. I don't watch baseball, but she loved the Red Sox. I told her before she went home I would wear her Red Sox hat and represent them here so long as she mentioned my name to Jesus when He passed by. I hope she's keeping up her end of the deal.

The limo driver retired and probably found a great deal on a used yellow truck.

Lex is still jumping big. He won the silver medal in the Rio de Janeiro Paralympics and the gold medal in the London World Paralympics Championships. Adam and I are still skydiving, but he goes more often than I do. Lex is planning on taking lessons and will be jumping with us soon. I know. I thought it was a bad idea too. Last one, best one.

I went back to the wax museum and they had turned it into a hot yoga studio. They didn't, of course, but I thought it would be pretty boss if I could tell you they did.

I still go to the pizza place, but these days I'm there for the food, not the tickets.

I still play the piano and hit lots of wrong notes, but my friends keep tapping their feet as if I didn't.

My eyesight hasn't come all the way back, but I continue to see more each day. I've gotten to know the new guy at TSA who took over for Adrian, and Karl is retiring from the attorney general's office after twenty years of navigating his faith in love.

I haven't been invited back to the White House, but that's okay.

Walter still meets people at the airport with his smile. I still get a dozen calls a week from jails and have plenty of prison socks if you need a pair.

I still carry my bucket around when I need to, which is most of the time. I haven't been to another crop drop, but next time I go, I'm filling my bucket with crocodiles and letting a couple loose in the room to see how fast our church can get up on the tables.

We're still meeting with witch doctors and enrolling them in our schools. The daughter of the head of the witch doctors enrolled in our high school. Parent-teacher conferences just got a lot more interesting. Oh, and the fingerprints on the cover of this book? I got the witch doctors in our school in Gulu together and most of the fingerprints are theirs.

One of the girls in our safe house in Uganda just started law school. She's our fourth Love Does student who is on the path to becoming a lawyer. They don't want to practice law; they want to do justice. There's a big difference between the two.

Kabi got sick and died unexpectedly. I'm kind of hoping we're not roommates when I get to heaven. Either way, because he found his way to the feet of Jesus, I expect to be spending a lot of time with him—but I still don't get it.

I keep asking Charlie where he wants to go, and thankfully he hasn't said Mount Kilimanjaro again. We did get some news I'm still trying to get my head around. He went in for an X-ray recently, and from what they discovered, it turns out there's a good chance he'll be able to be a father someday. I don't get that either—and neither do any of the surgeons who operated on him. He will be getting another restorative operation soon. It's nuts.

One thing has remained the same. Every time I wonder who I should love and for how long I should love them, God continues to whisper to me: *Everybody, always.*

See you on Tom Sawyer Island.

Bob

ACKNOWLEDGMENTS

As a kid, one of my favorite stories was the one about stone soup. You remember it. Travelers on a long journey stop in a village. They have nothing but a hunger in their bellies and a good idea. It wasn't just food they were hungry for, it was a desire to create community. What if all the very different people who live there could eat a meal together? At first, they got some pushback to their idea. I think I know why. Perhaps some people in the village had been raised to think food was scarce and they should hang on to what they had. *How could everybody actually be fed?* Others may have had disagreements with some of the villagers in the past or didn't understand why everybody needed to be invited. *Can't we just invite the popular ones or the ones who are easy to get along with? Be practical. How could we all sit at the same table together? Wouldn't there be arguments?* Still others, I imagine, had burned the toast more than once when they had tried to host a big meal. Or maybe when it was tried in the past no one showed, so why try again? Or maybe instead of a good meal, people thought they would get pressured to buy timeshares at a rundown resort.

Unafraid of the voices who disagreed with them and undeterred by all the reasons not to try, these travelers set up a pot in the middle of town. They invited anyone who believed in the idea to throw in a couple of carrots, some celery, onions—whatever they could offer. In the end, everybody was fed, but they got a lot more than food that day; they got each other.

Writing this book has been a feast, and there have been a lot of people who have thrown in the pot what they had. They didn't come with radishes and tomatoes; they came with love. The Cordon Bleu couldn't have set a more beautiful table. These pages contain the stories of some of my friends and what they've taught me about extravagant love and acceptance. I'm indebted to each one. The first thing I've learned from them is that I have a long way to go to be the kind of loving person I'm hoping I'll be some day. The second is that only the kind of radical love and acceptance I've experienced from them will help me close the distance. This is probably true for many of us.

There have been many cooks in the kitchen. Sweet Maria Goff, you continue to be one of my greatest teachers. You've helped me flip ideas like they were pancakes. Most of what I've gotten right about loving people is because I've seen you do it for the people around you.

Our kids and their spouses have been my teachers too. Lindsey, Jon, Richard, Ashley, Adam, thank you for letting me be your student. You've worked tirelessly to help me in every aspect of my life and, more importantly, have shown me a better, more beautiful way to live than I could have imagined myself.

My family and more than a few friends have also read these

words many times and helped me live out the best parts of them. When I got it wrong, they didn't scold me; they loved me and pointed me toward a better version of myself. They didn't just help me with punctuation. They reminded me of my purpose, too, which is to love everybody, not just the ones who are easy to be kind to.

To my eight people. You know who you are. Thank you for being closer than friends and for holding me close. You've poured unreasonable amounts of love into my life.

Bryan Norman, you've been a friend and trusted confidant. Thanks for helping me figure out which words to keep and which ones to scrape into the bin. To the many chefs at Thomas Nelson— Brian Hampton, Webster Younce, Janene MacIvor, Jeff James, Karen Jackson, Tiffany Sawyer, and the team—thank you for being endlessly patient with me as I gathered the groceries I'd need to make the soup. It's been a rare privilege to have the chance to write another book with you. To the massive number of new friends I've met in schools and cities in the past few years, thank you for making me feel welcome and for letting me hear your stories. You've reshaped how I experience my faith and see the world. The way you've loved people reminds me of the way Jesus did it.

To the team of people who help me daily get to where I'm supposed to be and have something to say when I get there, thank you. Dae, Becky, Haley, Tatave, and Jordan, you lead us with love and confidence and kindness. I also want to thank my trusted friend and advisor Jody Luke. You've brought truckloads of clarity and encouragement to all of us—but mostly to me.

To the courageous and hardworking crew at Love Does, the

mile-long parade of friends who make the work possible around the world, and to the more than one hundred teachers and thousands of kids in our schools, keep being brave and courageous and steadfast in your love for people who aren't like you. Don't give in to the pressure to be like each other; be like Jesus. You haven't backed down as you've fought for a better future for yourselves. Keep fighting for the people who haven't felt included yet—even if they creep you out. They are your brothers and sisters. Invite them to the party. If they say no, it's just because they're scared; invite them again.

Finally, Dad, thank you for being my friend and neighbor. I love you.

God doesn't give us a recipe for living as a community, but He gives us great ingredients: He gives us everybody, always. If we're going to get it right, it's going to take *everybody* to pull it off. It won't get done in a day or two either. It's going to take *always*.

ABOUT THE AUTHOR

Bob is the longest serving volunteer at Love Does and is its chief balloon inflator. He calls himself a "recovering lawyer" because after practicing law for almost thirty years, he walked into his own law firm and quit in order to pursue encouraging people full time. Bob is driven by a desire to love people and to motivate others to do the same. These days, you'll find Bob in an airport on his way to connect with and encourage people or, more likely, on his way home for supper with Sweet Maria.

A few years ago, Bob wrote a book called *Love Does*. He gave away all the proceeds from the book to help change the lives of children in countries where armed conflicts had left them vulnerable. Today, Love Does is an organization dedicated to helping kids in these areas including Iraq, Somalia, Uganda, Nepal, and India. You can find out more about Love Does at www.LoveDoes.org.

CONNECT WITH BOB

B ob's passion is people. He'd love to hear from you if you want to email him at info@bobgoff.com.

You can also follow him on Instagram and Twitter @bobgoff. Here's his cell phone number if you want to give him a call: (619) 985-4747.

Bob is also available to inspire and engage your team, organization, or audience. To date, he's spoken to more than one million people, bringing his unique perspective and exciting storytelling with him. He also puts on seminars called Dream Big. If you're interested in having Bob come to your event, check out bobgoff.com/speaking.